High Time for Reform: Drug Policy for the 21st Century

Edited by
Selina Chen and Edward Skidelsky

Social Market Foundation
December 2001

First published by The Social Market Foundation, 2001

The Social Market Foundation
11 Tufton Street
London SW1P 3QB

ISBN 1 874097 95 X

Cover and Design by
John and Michael Breeze

The Social Market Foundation

The Social Market Foundation, an independent think tank, explores ideas which link the state and the market to create the just, free and prosperous Britain of tomorrow.

The Foundation is a registered charity and a company limited by guarantee. It is independent of any political party or group and is financed by the sales of publications and by voluntary donations from individuals, organisations and companies.

The views expressed in publications are those of the authors and do not represent a corporate opinion of the Foundation.

CONTENTS

ACKNOWLEDGEMENTS

The editors would like to thank above all John McFadden, without whose generous financial support this book would never have been written.

They would also like to thank William McFadden and Pranay Sankletcha for their help with research, and Richard Davenport-Hines, Sarah Fitzpatrick, Phil Collins, Alastair Kilmarnock, Steven Knight, Donald McCarthy and Robert Skidelsky for their many helpful comments on the manuscript.

PREFACE

Over the past five years, a revolution has taken place in European drug policy. The Dutch experiment is well known to everyone; what is not so well known is that the same experiment is now being imitated by many other European states. In July 2001, the possession of drugs for personal use was removed from the criminal statutes of Portugal. The Belgian government resolved in January 2001 to decriminalise cannabis. In Spain and Italy, the possession of drugs for personal use has for many years been only an administrative offence. Discussion of decriminalisation is underway in Switzerland. 'User rooms', which provide safe conditions for the injection of heroin, have been established in Germany since 1994 and for several decades in the Netherlands. The creation of similar establishments is being debated in Luxembourg and Austria.

Britain has for some time lagged behind these developments on the continent. Our drug policy has preferred to borrow its rhetoric from America's War on Drugs. It is replete with 'Czars' and 'ten-year strategies'. The law has come increasingly adrift from public behaviour and public attitudes; it has become illegitimate and therefore unenforceable. The spread of recreational drug use, particularly among young people, and chiefly involving cannabis and Ecstasy, has robbed drug taking of much of its stigma. Enforcement - though not the law itself - has tended to follow suit, with the police using cautions rather than formal arrests and charges for possession of small amounts of cannabis and even other drugs.[1]

Until very recently politicians could count on strong public support for any anti-drugs measure. To appear 'tough on drugs' was a generally recognised political imperative. Perhaps the government was acting on this nostrum when it dismissed the Runciman Report. If so, it was a bad miscalculation. Not only the left-wing press, but even the conservative *Daily Mail* and *Daily Telegraph* condemned the reaction of the then Home Secretary, Jack Straw. 'For a government that prides itself on being so finely attuned to public opinion,' wrote *The Guardian*, 'the Blair team appears to have a tin ear for the debate on drugs.'[2]

Since then, the taboos surrounding the rational discussion of drugs have crumbled. The effect has been like that of *The Emperor's New Clothes*; every new breach of convention prompts further breaches. A recent example of this process was the Social Market Foundation's publication on July 6, 2001 of

Peter Lilley's call for the decriminalisation of cannabis (reprinted in this volume). Within a few days, Sir David Ramsbotham, the outgoing chief inspector of prisons, and former home secretaries Lord Jenkins and Lord Baker had all come out in favour of the proposal.

Finally, on 23 October, 2001, the Home Secretary David Blunkett indicated the government's willingness to reclassify cannabis as a Class C drug, the very proposal that, when suggested by the Runciman Report a year earlier, had been dismissed. He also hinted that the government may reconsider its guidelines on the prescription of heroin to addicts. These piecemeal accommodations to the public mood are preferable to total inaction, but they fall far short of the comprehensive and principled review of all aspects of drug policy that is so urgently required.

Blunkett has called for an 'adult, intelligent debate' on drugs – a call to which this collection of essays is a spirited response. Certainly, an open and public airing of arguments is necessary. The Runciman Report was a step in the right direction. It has helped create a freer climate for debate. But its recommendations were too cautious; they were constrained by what was perceived to be politically feasible at that time.

It is clear from the recent turn of events that a radical overhaul is both necessary and possible. Drug policy has for too long been based on ignorance and prejudice. It has pandered both to the popular mood and to international pressures. Changes in drug law have been introduced in piecemeal and opportunistic fashion; they have often been rushed and half-baked. A Royal Commission on Drugs, with a brief to examine all aspects of drug law and policy, is urgently required if we are to have a coherent and effective drugs policy for the 21st century. It would take only moderately courageous leadership to call one.

Robert Skidelsky
November 2001

INTRODUCTION

ROBERT SKIDELSKY

This collection of essays brings together writers from different intellectual and political backgrounds and from different nations. It shows how history, economics, sociology, medicine, philosophy – and, last but not least, personal experience – all have something to contribute to the debate. The essays express a range of different opinion; they are united only by their dissatisfaction with the status quo.

'Drugs' – an artificial category

The word 'drug' provides a good example of what Wittgenstein called 'the bewitchment of our intelligence by means of language'. It lumps together substances that have nothing whatsoever in common beyond the mere accident of illegality. Yet the application of the same word 'drug' to substances as different as cannabis, Ecstasy and heroin has given rise to the superstition that they share a natural affinity. This superstition lies behind what is known as the 'gateway effect' – the theory that cannabis 'leads on' to harder things.[3] Peter Lilley has little difficulty demonstrating that any such effect is an artefact of our legal system. Because cannabis is illegal it 'passes through the same illegal channels as hard drugs'. Buyers of cannabis are therefore in a position to obtain cocaine and possibly heroin as well. 'The ability of legalisation to break this link,' argues Lilley, 'is the most powerful argument in its favour'.

As Richard Davenport-Hines shows, it is a sheer accident of history that such a diverse group of substances has been so lumped together. Opium and cocaine, the two drugs whose prohibition is perhaps most justified, were first regulated under the 1916 Defence of the Realm Act. Wartime hysteria played a part in this decision, but the addictive potential of both substances was already well known. Cannabis was later prohibited in the erroneous belief that it was as dangerous as opium. The memorandum on the basis of which the decision was made described cannabis as 'a dangerous narcotic ... more harmful than opium.... About 70 per cent of insane people in lunatic asylums in Egypt are haschiche [sic] eaters or smokers.'[4] Once the category of 'dangerous drug' had been established in the public mind, it was easy to extend it. Amphetamine, LSD and Ecstasy were all outlawed in response to popular panic, long before anything was known of their true effects. As the most visible symbol of the permissive society, drugs were an easy scapegoat for everything that had gone wrong in the world. They became one of the great myths of the modern age.

Not only do the pharmacological effects of the various controlled drugs differ hugely; so also do their users. Geoffrey Pearson's essay shows that almost all the social problems commonly associated with 'drugs' are in fact bound up with just two substances: heroin and crack cocaine. Use of these two drugs is concentrated overwhelmingly in the poorest areas of Britain's cities, where it is implicated in numerous other social problems. Use of cannabis, Ecstasy and LSD, on the other hand, is not – as far as we know – concentrated among any particular social group. People increasingly discriminate between different forms of drug-use. A majority see cannabis as less harmful by far than other intoxicants, including alcohol and tobacco.[5] These changing attitudes are reflected in New Labour's strategy of targeting resources on those drugs that do the most damage. But this goal is impeded by the current law, which makes no distinction between substances as different as heroin, Ecstasy and LSD.

Drugs in a liberal society
The essays by Peter Lilley, Edward Skidelsky and Diana Gardner all take a principled stand on the question of drug legislation. They all strongly oppose the view that enforcing private morality is one of the proper functions of the state. The state, according to a long tradition of liberal argument, is not a moral institution. It should not try to impose on citizens a particular conception of how to live. Its purpose is simply to maintain justice and security. Beyond that, it must leave individuals free to pursue their own plan of life. This simple, powerful argument was one of the main forces behind the campaign against religious discrimination in the nineteenth century. It lies behind the campaign to end discrimination against homosexuals today. Why do we not extend the same liberty to drug users?

This liberal position does not entail the view that drug taking is perfectly safe. Even cannabis – the safest by far of all recreational drugs – is not without its risks. But the mere fact than an activity is dangerous does not constitute a reason for banning it, otherwise we would be sending people to jail for climbing mountains and racing motorbikes. Exactly *how* dangerous an activity must be before the law intervenes is a tough question; probably not all the contributors to this volume would agree with Edward Skidelsky's outright rejection of paternalism. But whatever the scope of paternalism, it is clear that cannabis falls outside it. The consistent verdict of medical science – cited here by Peter Lilley – is that it is less dangerous than tobacco and alcohol. The law is not only an ass; it is also a hypocrite.

Neither do proponents of the liberal approach necessarily *approve* of drug taking. But as Peter Lilley points out, the fact that an activity is considered immoral is not sufficient reason to ban it. 'Many things that are contrary to the prevailing moral code are not crimes. Most people consider adultery to be wrong. But we do not fine or jail adulterers.' The distinction between law and morality is one of the mainstays of the British liberal tradition. It is what distinguishes us from a country such as Iran, in which private vices are *ipso facto* criminal offences. Our policy has generally been to entrust the cultivation of virtue to civil institutions or to the individual. Devolving the guardianship of morals onto the state has always, and with good reason, been regarded with suspicion.

Addiction

The question then naturally arises: why are *any* drugs illegal? Why this glaring anomaly in our otherwise liberal political tradition? The answer, in a word, is addiction. The addictive potential of certain substances was the original reason for their prohibition, and the argument continues to carry force today. Addictive substances are thought to be too powerful to leave to the management of civil society. They are agents of enslavement. Liberal states do not allow an individual to sell himself into slavery; by parity of reasoning, they do not allow him to sell himself into the slavery of drug addiction.

But what exactly is addiction? Does it merit the lurid language in which it has so often been described? Some of the more radical libertarians deny that there is any such thing. Thomas Szasz argues, in terms reminiscent of Foucault, that addiction is a concept invented by the medical establishment to justify the extension of its own powers. 'Addictive drugs stand in the same sort of relation to ordinary or non-addictive drugs as holy water stands in relation to ordinary or non-holy water.'[6] For Szasz, the will holds no mysteries. So-called 'addicts' are simply people who enjoy taking drugs. There is something refreshingly robust about this view, but it is at complete variance with the experience of all those who have tried to give up nicotine or heroin. The phenomenon of addiction was recognised long before the nefarious 'medical establishment' even existed. The Italian rhetorician Pietro Della Valle wrote in 1622 that the Persians 'are so greatly addicted to the use of opium that it cannot be dispensed with; it being to them the greatest punishment to be obliged to abstain from it a single day.'[7]

James Bakalar and Diana Gardner both agree against Szasz that the term 'addiction' refers to a genuine condition. But it cannot be defined straightforwardly as 'loss of freedom' or 'slavery to habit'. Both authors show that 'free' and 'unfree' are not discrete and discontinuous states. There is, as James Bakalar puts it, no 'molecular switch in the brain that converts the merely reckless voluntary drug user into a diseased and unfree addict'. Freedom and unfreedom are merely the extreme poles of a continuum, between which ranges an infinity of gradations. It is along this range that the phenomenon of addiction lies. This means that addiction is an inherently vague concept, incapable of precise scientific definition. But vague concepts may be none the less indispensable. We do not abolish the words 'tall' and 'short' simply because we cannot indicate the precise point at which a short person becomes tall.

In an attempt to dispel the vagueness surrounding the concept of addiction, many writers have taken the short cut of simply identifying it with susceptibility to withdrawal symptoms. The appeal of this definition is that it is precise and physiological; addiction can be presented as a medical condition. But it is nonetheless fallacious. Stimulant drugs, many of them highly addictive, do not cause severe withdrawal reactions. And hospital patients who are prescribed opiates to relieve pain, even if they suffer withdrawal symptoms, rarely have any desire to go on taking the drug. Bakalar cites the well-known study of Lee Robins, which showed that the large majority of American soldiers addicted to heroin in Vietnam gave it up without difficulty on their return to the States. The threat of pain is not an insurmountable barrier to the exercise of free will. We can choose to suffer pain for the sake of some greater benefit; otherwise, as Gardner points out, no one would ever go to the dentist.

Addiction, then, is not a physiological so much as a psychological condition. Its distinguishing feature is persistent craving. But craving, no less than susceptibility to withdrawal symptoms, does not necessarily indicate a complete loss of freedom. There are a variety of techniques by means of which an addict can control or overcome his craving. These range from simple rules of thumb, such as avoiding the people with whom one used to take the drug, to sophisticated cognitive and behavioural therapies and the quasi-religious methods of Alcoholics Anonymous. All these techniques are alike in that they try to tap buried resources of will within the addict. They treat the addict as the agent of his own recovery, rather than as a mere object of medical management. Most addicts recover without the help of treatment, and most treatment is unsuccessful. Even when treatment is successful, it is not clear whether this not merely due to the prior resolve of the addict to come clean. There is some suspicion, as James Bakalar points out, that all treatments are just placebos.

It is often assumed that all addicts really want to quit, and are prevented from doing so only by the tenacious power of the drug. If this is correct, we may forcibly deny the addict his fix in order to help him realise his more fundamental desire for abstinence. We may, in Rousseau's famous words, 'force him to be free'. Diana Gardner argues that this way of describing the situation is misleading. The addict's desire to quit is countermanded not only by the power of the drug, but also by his desire to remain addicted. Addiction is experienced not merely as an alien force, but as something with which the addict at least partially identifies. The memoirs of many former addicts attest to this curious ambivalence. Addiction is described not merely as a slavery but also as a liberation. It is an escape from the restless drudgery of worldly concerns. 'The mortal boredom of the smoker who is cured!' writes Jean Cocteau. 'Everything one does in life, even love, occurs in an express train racing towards death. To smoke opium is to get out of the train while it is still moving. It is to concern oneself with something other than life, with death.'[8] The addictiveness of opiates is not merely an incidental hazard; it is an intrinsic part of their appeal. 'My addiction, such as it was, was chosen. Most are. For some of us, once you realise addiction is out there, you have to try it. ... Getting a habit isn't an accident, or the result of the 'power of the drug'; it's what you were after.'[9]

Another important piece of evidence against the traditional view of the addict as a 'slave to habit' is presented by Donald McCarthy. Were addiction a completely overwhelming desire for the drug in question, we would expect addicts to pay almost anything to obtain their fix. Addictive drugs would be – in the jargon – price inelastic; demand for them would be almost entirely insensitive to price. Yet this is not the case. The latest studies indicate that the price elasticity of heroin and cocaine is no less, and possibly greater, than the price elasticity of cigarettes. 'For cocaine, an increase of 1.0 per cent in price will decrease use by between 1.35 per cent and 2.0 per cent, while for heroin a 1.0 per cent increase in price is associated with a fall in use of between 1.0 per cent and 1.8 per cent.' These are, of course, only statistical aggregates. It is quite possible that they disguise considerable variation between the behaviour of addicts and non-addicts. Yet there is evidence that even addicts can moderate their consumption or abandon it altogether when the cost – financial, physical or moral – becomes too great. 'I used to shoplift, but I were scared o' doing shoplifting, scared o' getting caught,' said Wendy, a 21 year old Yorkshire addict interviewed by Geoffrey Pearson. 'And that stopped me from using... I wouldn't risk my liberty.'[10] And two addicts questioned by J. S. Blackwell said that they 'stopped using in order to get into shape for the football season.'[11]

Coming at the subject from very different angles, Bakalar, Gardner and McCarthy all end up presenting a remarkably similar picture of addiction. Medicine, philosophy and economics corroborate each other. The difference between addiction and non-addiction is one of degree, not of kind. The addict is not a zombie, a creature for whom the ordinary laws of motivation have been suspended. Addicts remain sensitive to all the usual pressures, only to a lesser degree. That is why most of them eventually manage to quit.

The case against coercive treatment
This has important implications for the way we treat addicts. Section 61 of the 1998 Crime and Disorder Act allows courts to order offenders convicted of drug-related crimes to undergo courses of treatment and compulsory testing. This is subject to the proviso that the offender gives his or her consent.[12] However, this proviso is less significant than it first appears, since the penalty for withholding consent, or for dropping out of the course once consent has been given, is usually imprisonment. This so-called 'coercive' treatment can only be justified on the assumption that addicts have an unambiguous desire to quit, and are prevented from acting on it only by the power of the drug. In this case, the courts are genuinely helping them realise their own 'true' will. They are 'forcing addicts to be free'. But if we agree with Gardner that in many cases the addict has no unambiguous desire to quit, then enforcing such treatment is 'not to liberate her; it is simply to impose on her an end that is not her own.' Bakalar agrees. 'Compulsory treatment for drug addiction is unjustified.'

Coercive treatment is often defended on grounds of utility. There is evidence from America that it may be as effective, if not more effective, than voluntary treatment.[13] This is a hotly disputed topic. In this volume, James Bakalar and Diana Gardner are sceptical about the efficacy of coercive treatment, whereas Geoffrey Pearson is more optimistic. But the question of utility is strictly secondary to the question of civil liberties. If coercive treatment is in effect a form of brainwashing, then the fact that it 'succeeds' is clearly no argument in its favour.

But the defender of coercive treatment needn't give up yet. Even if coercive treatment violates the addict's civil liberties, he might argue, it can still be justified on the grounds that without it the addict will continue to steal to finance his habit, thereby violating the civil liberties of others. This is the argument put forward by Geoffrey Pearson. But the reason the addict must steal to finance his habit is that government policy has put the price of heroin beyond his reach. Were heroin legally available, at reasonable prices, the addict would have no need to steal and the state no justification for forcing him into treatment. The state, in short, is justifying one wrong in terms of another. I will return later to this subject, when I examine the case for making heroin available on prescription.

The dangers of legalisation
But although the view of addiction outlined above supports a more humane and less coercive treatment of addicts, it does not support a policy of outright legalisation. Addiction – contrary to the claims of Thomas Szasz – is not merely a myth put out by the medical establishment. The word 'addiction' describes a genuine condition. It is one that we are all familiar with, even if we cannot give it a precise medical definition. Addiction involves, if not a total abnegation, then at least an impairment of autonomy. This alone is reason for treating heroin and cocaine differently from ordinary commodities.

The view of addiction outlined above also undermines one of the main tenets of the economic argument for legalisation. This is the hypothesis that legalisation would have little effect upon consumption. This is difficult to sustain. Not only does it ignore the greater ease of purchase, rise in quality and greater social respectability that legalisation would bring; it also ignores the fall in price. According to the reckoning of Richard Stevenson, himself a legaliser, the price of heroin in a free and legal market would be less than 3 per cent of what it is now.[14] The price of cocaine would fall by a similar order of magnitude. Given the fairly high price-elasticity of heroin and cocaine, we should therefore expect their use to increase dramatically upon legalisation.

Legalisation might, it is true, release countervailing forces. After legalisation, writes Stevenson, 'drug use would become less exciting and even boring'.[15] But this factor on its own cannot be expected to weigh very heavily against the massive fall in price and other costs. Taking a longer-term perspective, legalisation might release forces of social and moral disapproval that are currently 'crowded out' by the law. The institutions of civil society might be more effective in discouraging drug use than they are at present. Colombians are restrained from using cocaine, in spite of its low cost and easy availability, by powerful social taboos. But to legalise on this basis would be to take a massive gamble. Not all countries are as fortunate as Colombia. Iran, where heroin is equally cheap and plentiful, has an officially estimated one million addicts. If custom and religion have been unable to stop the use of heroin in Iran, they are hardly likely to succeed in Britain. Finally, the government could try to regulate the demand for drugs by taxing them. But it is questionable whether it could impose taxes sufficiently high to deter purchase, yet not so high as to make large-scale smuggling profitable.[16] Taxation might prevent consumption from rising to its 'natural' level, but it would not be able to prevent it from rising considerably above its current level.

But this does not dispose of the legaliser's argument, if the purpose of policy is to reduce not the quantity of drugs consumed but the injury to health. Most of the risks ascribed to heroin are attributable to factors connected with its illegality; the variable purity of street heroin is the main cause of overdosing, and shared needles are a major cause of HIV and hepatitis infection. During the Swiss experiment with heroin prescription, recounted here by Ingo Pies and Claudia Schott, the number of deaths from overdosing dropped to zero. But even pure, properly administered heroin is dangerous. Many overdoses result not from an unexpectedly strong fix of heroin, but from a sudden and mysterious loss of tolerance.[17] And the psychological effects of chronic heroin use are not yet fully understood. The legalisation of heroin would probably replace a small number of very sick addicts with a much larger number of moderately sick addicts. Given that we cannot predict the exact scale of the increase, nor do we know the precise effects of pure as opposed to street heroin, any cost-benefit analysis of legalisation is impossible. Once again, it seems a foolish gamble to take.

The failure of enforcement
The latest findings on the price-elasticity of heroin and cocaine have also given ammunition to the proponents of supply-side policy. If raising street price can reduce consumption, they argue, then the efforts of the law-enforcement bodies are not in vain. This argument is usually associated with the American

'war on drugs', but it has also been influential here in Britain. In the year 2001–2002, the government plans to spend £373 million on measures designed to reduce the availability of drugs. This is the largest single item in the drugs budget.

Donald McCarthy presents powerful economic reasons for believing that this money is misspent. If enforcement measures *did* raise the street price of heroin and cocaine, they might indeed be successful in reducing consumption. But there is no evidence that they do. Despite the massive increase in expenditure on crop-eradication, interdiction, policing and incarceration, the price of heroin and cocaine on the streets of America continues in its 'secular decline'. Policies directed at the upper end of the supply chain, at the production and smuggling stages, are, argues McCarthy, particularly futile. A campaign against low-level dealers is more likely to have an impact. Yet it is precisely this latter policy that is ethically least acceptable. There is little sympathy for big drug-barons. But most street-level heroin dealers are themselves addicts. They are forced to deal because prohibition keeps the price of heroin artificially high. To force such people into crime and then to punish them for it seems monstrously unfair. Prohibitionists, as Ingo Pies and Claudia Schott point out, are caught in a bind. Prohibition can only work if it is inhumane; all attempts to humanise it succeed only in blunting its efficacy.

The case for prescription

If prohibition has failed, yet legalisation is a dangerous gamble, it seems wisest to go for a compromise. This is the tactic adopted by Ingo Pies and Claudia Schott in this book. The current law, as Pies and Schott point out, represents a huge sacrifice of the interests of addicts to those of potential addicts. Addicts are condemned to a life of crime and disease *pour encourager les autres*. The essay in this volume by Ian McLaughlin, a prisoner and former heroin addict, spells out precisely what this involves. What McLaughlin detested most about his periods of heroin addiction was not dependence on the drug itself, but enthralment to the criminals who supplied him. 'The worst thing was falling into the clutches of the dealers. On the first occasion I tried to finance my addiction by moving up the pyramid, but very quickly found I couldn't bring myself to inflict on others the misery I was inflicting on myself. On the second occasion I allowed my debt to build up until it was out of control.'

It is often assumed that the misery of addicts is a necessary price to pay for the ultimate goal of keeping consumption down. But Pies and Schott demonstrate that this is by no means the case. A policy of *prescribing* heroin to addicts would serve the interests of both addicts and non-addicts. It would protect non-addicts against the temptation of addiction by putting legal heroin beyond their reach. And it would preserve the health and dignity of addicts by making heroin available to them at low cost under controlled conditions. McLaughlin emphatically agrees with this solution. 'I now firmly believe that *all* illegal drugs must be decriminalised, for the sake of the huge number of drug users and the victims they create. Drugs *must* be taken out of the hands of criminal suppliers. They should be made available on prescription, at affordable prices, to all users.'

Prescription would not only not increase the availability of heroin to non-addicts; it might actually *decrease* it. Because many addicts deal to fund their addiction, prescription would destroy the pyramid structures that are the mainstay of the illicit drug market. Prescription would also eliminate the acquisitive crime to which addicts at present resort. One study put the total value of drug-related theft in 1993 at £1,999 million, or about half the total value of theft in that year.[18] A policy of prescription would decimate that figure at little cost to the Exchequer. Finally, prescription would drastically reduce the burden that drug addicts at present place on the NHS.

Ingo Pies and Claudia Schott recount some of the successes of the Swiss prescription experiment. During the period of the experiment, the percentage of overdoses among total fatalities dropped to zero. (The equivalent percentage in Germany is 72.) The total saving to society, including the savings from reduced crime rates, improved health and improved productivity, amounted to 95.50 Swiss francs (roughly £53 at 1996 rates) per addict per day. The official report on the experiment concluded that 'significant improvements can be obtained in terms of health and lifestyle, and these persist even after the end of treatment.... The economic benefit of heroin-assisted treatment is considerable, particularly due to the reduction in the costs of criminal procedures and imprisonment and in terms of disease treatment.'[19] These findings were later endorsed, with some qualifications, by the World Health Organisation.[20] A recent follow-up study confirmed that heroin-assisted treatment treatment was more cost-effective than well-designed methadone-maintenance treatment, with patients often showing 'great improvements in medical and social variables, including criminality.'[21]

One of the greatest tragedies of recent British drug policy was the closure of Dr. John Marks's famous Chapel Street Clinic in Merseyside. One of the last remnants of the traditional 'British system' of heroin prescription, Dr. Marks's clinic supplied free heroin and cocaine to addicts from 1982 to 1995. No official survey of the clinic was ever carried out, but the evidence of its success is nevertheless remarkable. A local police study showed a roughly 15-fold reduction in the rate of conviction among the clinic's patients.[22] An estimated £5000 per week was removed from the local black economy.[23] And the incidence of overdosing and HIV infection among patients dropped to zero. Visitors to the clinic were astonished to find that Dr. Marks's patients did not look at all like the traditional image of junkies. 'They were well dressed, talkative, energetic – they had jobs – and they used heroin daily.'[24] The patients themselves were enthusiastic. 'For the first time in ten years I had spare time,' said one addict Juliette. 'I didn't have to worry that my dealer wouldn't show – I didn't have to worry about the price or where to steal the money.'[25] A 1997 report commissioned by the Australian National Drug Crime Prevention Fund and the Tasmania Police concluded that the project had been a success and recommended that it be used as a model for trials in Australia.[26] The trials never took place, for political reasons.

Under strong pressure from America, the Chapel Street Clinic was shut down in April 1995. The official explanation was cost cutting: heroin is more expensive than the preferred substitute methadone. All of John Marks's 450 patients were transferred to the local methadone clinic. A spate of deaths followed. Many former patients returned to crime. 'I have seen people who were on heroin maintenance out of court', said Cheshire probation officer Chris Walsh. 'This was taken away and they were put on methadone. I've seen them back in court. As simple as that – they were kept away from criminal activity and now they are back.'[27]

No investigation into the relative effectiveness of different forms of treatment was carried out during this period, despite numerous requests from researchers in England and elsewhere. Such a study was commissioned only *after* the Chapel Street Clinic was shut down. The preferred methadone treatment system was thus able to avoid any embarrassing comparisons. Methadone is now almost the only the only legally available opiate in Britain; less than 1 per cent of maintenance clients receive heroin. Yet the superiority of methadone over heroin has never been proven. Indeed, there are good reasons for thinking that heroin must be superior. Methadone does not fully relieve the craving for heroin, so most addicts on methadone programmes continue to use heroin on the side.[28] Methadone has many unpleasant side effects. It is at least as dangerous as heroin; according to some estimates, it is more dangerous. Dr Russell Newcombe estimates that 'methadone contributes to the overdose deaths of significant numbers of opiate users – more than heroin does both in absolute numbers and death rates per estimated 10,000 users'.[29] For all these reasons, many heroin addicts prefer to remain on the black market than to join methadone clinics. Heroin has certain technical disadvantages compared to methadone; its effects are shorter lasting, so it needs to be administered more frequently. But this in itself hardly constitutes a reason for not considering heroin prescription. Only the irrational stigma that attaches to it can explain why heroin has never been given another chance.

In spite of the evidence in favour of heroin prescription, there remains one serious worry. Wouldn't a policy of prescribing heroin only to addicts give casual users a perverse incentive to *become* addicts? At the very least, it would remove any very serious *disincentive* to becoming an addict. It would thus undermine the original reason for keeping heroin illegal, namely, to keep total consumption to a minimum. Wouldn't a policy of prescription create a hoard of state-subsidised drug-addicts? The problem – essentially the same problem that bedevils all forms of welfare provision – is that of moral hazard. It deserves to be taken seriously.

Yet there are two good reasons for thinking that prescription wouldn't lead to a huge increase in heroin addiction. The first is the effect it would have on the black market, analysed here by Pies and Schott. Most dealers are also addicts. They sell in order to finance their own habit. If they could be persuaded to receive heroin on prescription, at an affordable price, they would no longer have any reason to sell to others. The pyramid structure that drives the illegal market would be destroyed. Criminal gangs, unable to compete with the state, would increasingly turn to other, more profitable commodities. These speculations are born out by data from heroin clinics. Sue Edwards, a social worker at the Clwyd Drug Service, reported that prior to the prescription of heroin there had been an organised black market in the region. 'She actively targeted dealers, particularly user/dealers, and was successful in getting them onto a prescription. She says that this removed their need to deal on a day-to-day basis because a) they now had the drug of their choice so they no longer needed to deal; b) the chance of losing the guaranteed daily dosage was too great a risk to take; and c) sheer economics told them that the market had disappeared.'[30] Dr. John Marks claims that Widnes, the Merseyside town in which his clinic was located, saw a 12-fold decline in the incidence of addiction following the introduction of prescription.[31] More research needs to be done to confirm these claims, but they are nonetheless suggestive.

The second reason for thinking that prescription wouldn't lead to a huge increase in drug addiction is psychological. Taking out a prescription allows the addict to resume a more or less normal life. His chances of holding down a permanent job and a stable relationship are greatly increased. His contact with the drug scene is severed. The clinic provides him with counselling. These changes put the addict in a much stronger position to quit, should he so wish. They create a 'virtuous circle'. Dependence on the black market, on the other hand, creates a vicious circle. As the addict is driven further into poverty and crime, all sources of satisfaction other than the drug become increasingly inaccessible. Eventually, he reaches the stage where he has nothing else to live for. The black market *entrenches* addiction. Once again, these speculations are born out by the data. By the end of the Swiss experiment, 'a total of 83 people had decided to give up heroin and switch to abstinence therapy. The probability of this switch to abstinence therapy grew as the duration of individual treatment increased.'[32]

Many further question marks hang over prescription. There are ongoing debates about the best method of dispensing the drug (as a powder to be injected intravenously or in a cigarette). The danger of prescription heroin or cocaine leaking onto the black market is a serious one. But a police exercise conducted over a six-month period in 1987 by the Liverpool drug squad found no arrested drug takers in possession of prescription drugs to which they were not authorised.[33] They drew the conclusion that there was little leakage of licit heroin onto the black market. (Methadone, on the other hand, is regularly sold on. This is unsurprising, given that most methadone patients carry on using black market heroin.[34]) But if the risk of leakage is still felt to be too high, it can be simply averted by requiring patients to take their dosage in the clinic. This was the rule followed in Switzerland, with universal success. Cocaine raises problems of its own. Whereas heroin addicts require their fix with a clockwork regularity, cocaine addicts tend to binge and then abstain. This might create problems for regular prescription. However, Dr. Marks prescribed cocaine cigarettes with reported success. More research needs to be done.

All these problems require careful consideration. But none of them constitutes a fundamental objection to the principle of heroin and cocaine maintenance. The best argument in favour of prescription is the failure of the alternatives. The number of addicts in Britain has risen geometrically – at least until 1996, the year when the Addicts Index ceased to be maintained. But recent surveys indicate no modification of the general upward trend, and a worrying increase in juvenile heroin use.[35] In the face of such failure, the government would do well to consider alternatives.

Conclusion

If there is one thing that unites all the essays in this book, it is dissatisfaction with the current state of drug law and drug law enforcement. There is a general recognition that most of the problems attributed by politicians to drug *use* in fact spring directly from drug *policy*. 'Prohibition,' as Pies and Schott put it, 'not part of the solution; it is part of the problem.'

Of the many anomalies in current drug law, the prohibition of cannabis stands out most glaringly. Peter Lilley, Geoffrey Pearson and Edward Skidelsky all call for some form of decriminalisation or legalisation. The reclassification of cannabis as a Class C drug, the reform proposed by the Runciman Report and cautiously endorsed by David Blunkett, is an unsatisfactory half-way house. It will do nothing to regulate the illegal market in cannabis, and, most importantly, will keep wide open the 'legal gateway' leading to harder drugs. This is the single most powerful argument for outright legalisation.

Outside government circles, the decriminalisation of cannabis is no longer particularly controversial. Serious public debate on hard drugs has, on the other hand, hardly begun. Yet it is precisely here that reform could have most influence for the good. One of the main ideas to emerge from this volume is the prescription of heroin to addicts. Gardner, McLaughlin, Pies and Schott all put this forwards as a solution to the current crisis.

Pushed into the background by the current 'war on terrorism' are important indications that the government is reconsidering its policy on prescription. In his 23 October speech, Blunkett revealed that '...with the Department of Health we will produce new guidance for heroin prescribing. This will work towards providing a bridge between those who are obtaining heroin illegally, often through criminal activity, and the methadone treatment prescribing.' This change in policy is welcome, although the manner of its announcement was regrettably underhand. Heroin prescription should not be sneaked in through the back door, but should be made, as in Switzerland, the subject of a public and nationwide trial.

PART I
History and Principles

1. THE HISTORY OF BRITISH DRUG LAW

RICHARD DAVENPORT-HINES

The Misuse of Drugs Act of 1971 is obsolete. It was framed at a time when politicians of all parties were highly resistant to the notion that illicit drug use was related to social deprivation, urban decay and poor employment opportunities. It was framed before knowledge of the action of drugs on the brain had reached its present advanced state. It was framed many years before most European governments, if not the United States, accepted that the spread of AIDS among intravenous drug users necessitated strategies of harm minimisation rather than absolute suppression. The 1971 Act was the creation of Edward Heath's government, which – despite an early rhetorical commitment to restoring the power of market forces – spent its years in office trying to restrain them. The ideological revolution of the Thatcher years has led to the reinstatement of market mechanisms in most areas of the economy. The trade in drugs remains one significant exception. Our law against drugs recalls the old communist law against 'profiteering' and, like that law, it creates irresistible incentives for entrepreneurs willing to break it.

Although the shortcomings of the 1971 Act are widely acknowledged, its historical antecedents are little known. These deserve careful scrutiny before the Act is reformed. British legislation covering the misuse of drugs is highly distinctive in many of its features. Knowing its history helps us both to understand why it has failed and to avoid these failures in the future.

Two distinct trends in British drug legislation can be distinguished. International agreements and treaties provided the original impetus for domestic drug control. Many of the key developments were initiated at conferences in The Hague, Geneva and Vienna. The formative years of these controls lay between 1912 and 1961. 'At the center of this... universe lay governments, enforcement agencies, international organs, and pharmaceutical interests. Control officials rarely considered issues of demand, had little knowledge about addicts, and seldom examined the relationship between regulatory measures and illicit activity. Control advocates believed that if only the rules could be drawn properly, and if only governments carried out their obligations, the problem would recede.'[36] In the period since 1961, British legislation has continued to reflect international obligations. United Nations conventions oblige Britain to make the possession of various specified substances a criminal offence.

However, a further trend emerged in 1964 and has persisted ever since. Beginning with the Douglas-Home administration, successive governments have tried to win popularity with electorates by introducing high-profile laws directed against drug use and drug trafficking. This legislation has been populist in inspiration; it has sometimes run counter to the expert opinion of the time. Usually it has been framed to impress the middle-aged with good intentions rather than to deter the young with convincing arguments. Overall, it has failed.

Before prohibition

Public opinion has always mattered in questions of drug misuse. Indeed, during the nineteenth century, public disapproval constituted the main form of regulation. The assessment of a person's drug habit depended largely upon his or her general behaviour. The heavy laudanum abuse of King George IV was widely despised, because it was seen to exemplify a luxurious and spendthrift character. But there was no contempt for Wilkie Collins, despite his reliance on laudanum and occasionally morphine, because he worked hard. Gladstone took nips of laudanum before public speaking and was thought none the worse for it; his sister's addiction to morphine, coupled as it was with erratic behaviour, led to ostracism. The many middle-class women who became dependent in mid-century on hypodermic injections of morphine were regarded as having a nervous disease (neuralgia) even when, as occasionally happened, they lied or stole in furtherance of their habit. They were thought of as tiresome rather than criminal or vicious. But most Victorian opiate addicts avoided stigma, because they controlled their habits and did not put their jobs or domestic stability in jeopardy.

As to the retailing of drugs, a regime of voluntary self-regulation was maintained by successive Pharmacy Acts. The Pharmacy Act of 1852 set up a Register of Pharmacists, but imposed few other effective restrictions on the supply of drugs. A subsequent Pharmacy Act of 1868, administered by the Pharmaceutical Society, introduced controls on the supply of opium. The sale of opium preparations by general dealers was prohibited, and was henceforth confined to pharmacists. But consumers who could afford the physician's fees had no difficulty in obtaining their opium on prescription, and it required little ingenuity for poorer people to evade the spirit of this legislation. It was generally believed that anyone determined to obtain opiates could do so. However, recent research by Joseph Spillane concludes that in the USA by the

1890s druggists 'claimed the right to refuse cocaine sales on the basis of the consumer's social status or race', and that outside of vice districts and other marginal areas of American towns and cities pharmacists exercised strict self-regulation in their supply of cocaine.[37] It is likely that many British pharmacists exercised similar discrimination in supplying customers with certain commodities.

The dawn of prohibition
The end of individual national systems of regulation began with the annexation of the Philippines by the USA in 1898. The Americans prohibited opium smoking, popular among the Chinese inhabitants, and suppressed their opium 'dens'. They were dismayed when these policies resulted in a spread of opium smoking from the Chinese community to the Filipino population in general. There had been no smuggling before prohibition; it was henceforth an ineradicable problem.[38] The American response was to convene an international conference in Shanghai in 1909, with the purpose of tackling opium smoking in China and the Far East as a whole. In order to avoid accusations of hypocrisy, Congress passed the first major piece of federal drug legislation, the Smoking Opium Exclusion Act of 1909. By suppressing opium smoking, this act was recognised by medical experts to have begun the fashion for taking heroin instead.[39]

The international sequel to Shanghai was the Hague Opium Conference of 1911-12, presided over by the U.S. Episcopalian Bishop of the Philippines. The European powers tried to resist the extensive prohibitionist proposals tabled by the U.S. delegation, but the Hague Convention of 1912 was nevertheless far-reaching. It established the first international regulatory system for any commodity. The signatory powers committed themselves to limiting the manufacture, trade and use of opiates and cocaine to medical purposes. The Convention obliged them to close opium 'shops', to penalise unauthorised possession of opiates and to prohibit their sale to unauthorised persons. The implementation of this convention by Britain and the other European powers was delayed by the outbreak of war in 1914 and finally accomplished only in the early 1920s.

The Hague Conference was of high significance. Sir William Collins MP, who was a British delegate, wrote, 'the [drugs] problem was rapidly passing out of the limitations of the "Far East"... and was becoming a question of world-wide importance.' He also discerned a new punitive and penal spirit, spreading to

Europe from the USA. Among some delegates at The Hague there had been 'a disposition... to regard the morphinist and the cocainist merely as invalids and objects of pity', but Collins and the prohibitionists disagreed. 'Many of them are social pests of the most dangerous kind. Bankrupt of moral sense and will-power, they are lying and deceitful, prodigal of time, plausible to a degree, backbiting and contentious, prone to vice and apt for crime.'[40] This characterisation of the addict as vicious and criminal was reinforced in the USA by such federal legislation as the Harrison Act of 1914, and the Supreme Court decision of 1919 that physicians should not provide maintenance prescriptions for addicts. Americans with drug habits were cut off from medical support, and were obliged to obtain supplies from illicit sources. Criminal gangs began trafficking, and prisons filled with drug offenders.[41]

Drug prohibition spread to Britain during the First World War. In 1916, the wartime Defence of the Realm Act was extended to cover cocaine and opium. Under Regulation 40(B) of this act the supply of dangerous drugs to troops became a criminal offence, as did their possession by a civilian without a medical prescription. Regulation 40(B) prohibited the import of cocaine and opiates except under license, and their supply by a pharmacist except under prescription. The regulation was made at the request of the Commissioner of the Metropolitan Police, who was concerned by reports that Soho prostitutes were supplying cocaine to their soldier clients. Sir Malcolm Delevingne of the Home Office, the most influential figure in British drugs policy in the first half of the twentieth century, described Regulation 40(B) as 'an emergency measure based upon the known evil existing among, at any rate, a section of the troops.' Although there was not 'an assumed prevalence among the general population', this evil 'could only be stopped by a *general* restriction.'[42] The prohibition of heroin and cocaine was thus not intended to be permanent. Like so many other wartime restrictions, however, it was never to be repealed.

International pressures

In accordance with British obligations under the Hague Convention of 1912, the first Dangerous Drugs Act was enacted in 1920. This legislation, together with additional Dangerous Drugs Acts of 1923, 1925 and 1932 'sprang', in Delevingne's words, 'directly out of International Agreements.... They were passed by Parliament in order to give effect to the obligations into which, by the ratification of those agreements, Great Britain had entered... it is the honourable tradition of this country to fulfil its engagements.'[43] International diplomatic agreements have continued to the present day to dictate British drug law.

Because British drug legislation had its origins in international agreements, it often received only cursory parliamentary consideration. The 1920 Act, for example, limited the manufacture, sale, possession and distribution of cocaine and opiates to authorised persons. It required that the movement of drugs between manufacturer, supplier and consumer be documented in registers available for official inspection. The import and export of such drugs was brought under Home Office regulation. The Act created the new offence of being the occupier of premises permitting the smoking of prepared opium. It also controlled the import, export and manufacture of tinctures of cannabis, although it did not prohibit the drug's possession. Yet despite these far-reaching provisions, the bill was debated by only six speakers in the House of Commons and the discussion was framed in mediocre generalities.

This legislative carelessness is particularly patent in the case of cannabis. The Home Office did not at first want to legislate, but foresaw that the prevalence of hashish in Egypt, despite decades of prohibition there, might require the 'international regulation of the drug.'[44] Indeed, shortly afterwards the Egyptian Ministry of Interior concluded that as it was 'impossible to keep hashish out of Egypt', the best solution was that 'the League of Nations should consider hashish as an international affair and should try to persuade its members to make dealing in or consuming the drug a crime punishable by severe penalties.' At the Geneva Conference on Opium of 1924-25, the Egyptian delegate proposed bringing hashish within the Hague Convention. The memorandum circulated in support of his proposal described hashish as 'a dangerous narcotic... more harmful than opium.... About 70 per cent of insane people in lunatic asylums in Egypt are haschiche [sic] eaters or smokers.'[45] Congressman Stephen Porter, leader of the U.S. delegation, supported this initiative. 'We are asking them to help us to destroy the vice of opium, coca leaves and their derivatives. This is a good time to practice a little reciprocity. They have their troubles and we have ours.'[46]

The British, Canadian and Dutch delegations hesitated to agree 'because it was uncertain at that time whether there was a potential... medical value in cannabis',[47] but finally the contracting powers at the Geneva Conference agreed in 1925 to prohibit the import and export of Indian hemp except for certified medical or scientific purposes. In Britain, cannabis was immediately rescheduled as a poison. A few months later, the Dangerous Drugs Act of 1925 brought British law into line with the Geneva Convention. The House of Commons debate on 5 August 1925 lasted less than five minutes; Indian hemp, or cannabis, was not mentioned once. The House of Lords debate was slightly longer. Peers followed the advice of Lord Haldane that as it was 'impossible to form any judgement on the details of the Bill' it should 'be taken by the House to a large extent on trust.'[48] It was on this slipshod basis that the possession of cannabis was criminalised.[49]

After the war, the internationalisation of drugs policy continued apace. The Geneva Protocol of 1946 transferred the League of Nations' drugs functions to the United Nations Commission on Narcotics Drugs (CND). CND was from the outset dominated by the United States. The head of the Federal Bureau of Narcotics, Harry Anslinger, attempted to turn it into a personal stronghold. In 1948, he launched a plan for a single, worldwide convention on narcotic drugs. As an interim measure, an international opium protocol was agreed in 1953. The protocol incorporated severe controls on poppy and coca production, and stipulated that opium should be restricted to medical and scientific use. These measures reflected the American policy of the preceding 45 years. In the years that followed, many signatories found the protocol so impractical and over-zealous that they determined not to ratify its terms. It was indicative of a counter-reaction to American hegemony that the CND was in 1955 relocated from New York to Geneva despite strenuous opposition from the Federal Bureau of Narcotics. Anslinger indeed boycotted the CND meetings of 1956 and 1958, held in Geneva rather than New York.

British legislation continued to reflect international obligations. In 1955, Britain responded to the Opium Protocol by introducing legislation prohibiting the manufacture, distribution and medical use of heroin. The Eden government was, however, defeated by a rebellion in the House of Lords. The British Medical Association had campaigned to retain the use of heroin in medicine, and many peers supported them. Several speakers in the Lords and contributors to the medical press argued that the American experience of heroin prohibition had proved a failure and that the British should not repeat the mistake.[50] However, British export licenses for heroin were not issued after 1956.

Harry Anslinger's vision of a worldwide convention on narcotic drugs was finally realised in the Single Convention of 1961. The Single Convention forms the basis of current international drug law. Signatories are committed to limitations on the cultivation, manufacture, importation and possession of drugs as well as to requirements of labelling, record keeping, prescribing and secure storage. Breaches of the convention by citizens of signatory states are stipulated to be punishable offences, with imprisonment among the punitive options. The 1961 Convention has been cited by a succession of home secretaries as laying an obligation upon the British legislature to penalise the misuse of drugs. In truth, the Convention never specified that signatory states create or maintain criminal offences relating to drugs. This obligation was imposed only as recently as 1988, under the United Nations Convention on Illicit Traffic in Narcotic Drugs and Psychotropic Substances. But as the Dutch and other European legislatures have demonstrated, there is more room for manoeuvre under these conventions than the Home Office has found it expedient to acknowledge. The 1988 Convention, for example, states that the criminal offences of possession, purchase or cultivation for personal *consumption* are subject to the signatory powers' constitutional and legal systems. This would permit a wide range of legal reforms, if not for trafficking offences then at least for offences involving personal consumption.

But it is informal contacts with American drug enforcement agencies, rather than the direct pressure of international treaty obligations, that have had the most influence on British policy since the mid-1960s. This influence was strongest during the Reagan-Thatcher years. The second term of the Thatcher government saw a flurry of drugs legislation, much of it modelled on the American policy of 'getting tough' with traffickers. The Controlled Drugs Act of 1985 increased the maximum penalty for trafficking to life imprisonment, and the Drug Trafficking Offences Act of 1986 introduced measures to confiscate the assets of drugs traffickers. And the Thatcher government's hard-line attitude to cannabis derived support from the American 'gateway' theory – the theory that cannabis leads inexorably to harder drugs. Ironically, in view the general tendency of the eighties, illegal drugs were never regarded as commodities subject to market forces. Economic liberalism marched hand in hand with social conservatism.

The mimicking of American policies often had absurd consequences. One notorious example was the inflammatory warning against crack cocaine delivered by a representative of the Drug Enforcement Agency to a conference of British police officers 1989. This led to the formation of a national task force on crack and a rhetorical report by the House of Commons Home Affairs Committee. There was so little for the police task force to do that it was disbanded after a year. But there was little acknowledgement of the reason that crack cocaine did not escalate in Britain as it had in the United States. This was chiefly the result of market conditions: crack could not compete, in terms of price or availability, with the established supply of amphetamines in British towns and cities.[51]

Britain continues to be more influenced by American drug policy than any other European country. The 1998 appointment of Keith Hellawell as 'Drug Czar' was a direct echo of American practice. And New Labour has been unable to resist the political capital to be gained from hasty reactions to drug scare stories emanating from across the Atlantic. Its response to the 'date rape' drug Rohypnol is a case in point. Rohypnol received disproportionate and often misleading publicity in the United States during 1996. The Rohypnol panic reached Britain in December 1997, and despite the spuriousness of much of the press excitement and the speculative nature of police advice, statutory controls were imposed in May 1998. Unauthorised possession (without prescription) of Rohypnol became a criminal offence subject to a maximum penalty of two years' imprisonment, or an unlimited fine, or both.[52] However, recent developments in New Labour's drug policy seem to suggest a distancing from the American line and an increasing interest in European 'harm reduction' approaches. These developments can only be welcomed.

The politicisation of drug policy

But British drug legislation no longer takes its cue entirely from international developments. Since the early sixties, it has increasingly been framed in response to domestic pressure. The crucial change has been the rise of the modern 'drug culture', associated with youthful rebellion and sexual liberation. How much drug use actual escalated during the sixties is open to dispute. Figures suggest that the rise in British cannabis, heroin and amphetamine consumption began much earlier, around 1950. But it was during the sixties that illegal drug use by young people became an object of mass anxiety. Drugs became a convenient symbol for everything that was going wrong in society. Taking a 'hard stand' on drugs became, for politicians, a watermark of sound moral values. A new political consensus was established. Few have been brave enough to buck it.

The first post-war British drug law passed in response to domestic pressure was the Drugs Act of 1964, which introduced controls over amphetamines. This law was prepared in response to a hint from the incoming Prime Minister Sir Alec Douglas-Home to his Home Secretary Henry Brooke, and was hurried through parliament just before the general election to show that the government was in earnest about 'purple hearts'. The act was directed against young amphetamine users and the clubs and cafés where they congregated, but ignored the many unhappy housewives who were known to be abusing amphetamines. It included no controls on manufacture, distribution and records of sales, and did not prevent over-prescription by physicians. The press claimed, falsely, that the law was directed against mods and rockers. (Such evidence as is available suggests that there was minimal amphetamine use in seaside towns in 1964, but that consumption rose sharply after legislation.)[53]

A comparable intervention was the Drugs Act Modification Order of 1966, which made the unlicensed possession of LSD a criminal offence. LSD had been used in psychiatric medicine from the early 1950s, but its provocative use after 1960 by Dr. Timothy Leary and others had resulted in the decision to bring it under the control of the U.S. Federal Drug Administration and to repress its use in psychiatric medicine. When these controls came into force in 1963, the drug immediately started appearing on the streets of American cities and the soaring fashion for LSD took off. British criminal sanctions against LSD were influenced as much by aversion to Californian hippies as by the dangers of the drug itself. As in America, they had the unintentional effect of escalating use. Before 1966, consumption of LSD had largely been confined to a minority of Oxbridge undergraduates. After 1966, the quality of the drug deteriorated but levels of consumption rose sharply. By making profits available to criminal suppliers, the law against LSD led to an organised and ambitious black market. When consumption of the drug in Britain finally declined in the seventies, it was less as the result of police operations such as 'Operation Julie' than changing drug fashions among young people: LSD became derided as 'hippie shit'.[54]

The victory of Nelson Rockefeller in the hard-fought 1966 election for the New York governorship was widely attributed to his commitment – never fulfilled – to 'sweep addicts off the streets'. This was the first occasion in which drugs became a decisive electoral factor. In Britain, too, drug policy became a matter of political calculation. This was evident by 1968, when an official advisory committee, chaired by Baroness Wootton of Abinger, endorsed the opinion of the Indian Hemp Commission of 1893-94 and the New York Mayor's Committee on Marijuana of 1944 that the long-term consumption of cannabis in moderation was not harmful, and that cannabis did not lead inexorably to the use of more dangerous drugs. The members of this committee were distinguished experts of irreproachable rectitude. Their report was widely misrepresented as demanding the immediate legalisation of cannabis and they were insulted in the press and parliament. The Home Secretary, James Callaghan, playing to the gallery, rejected the committee's recommendations: 'I am glad if my decision has enabled the House to call a halt to the advancing tide of so-called permissiveness.' He claimed that the Wootton sub-committee had been 'over-influenced' by a 'lobby... in favour of legalising pot'. Dismissing expert advice, he appealed instead to 'public opinion'.[55]

The role of the press in fomenting public fears about drugs has always been enormous. As early as the thirties, the Home Office was aware of being under pressure to respond to press agitation. Since the mid-sixties, the pressure on politicians has been overwhelming. In 1970, Richard Crossman described the Home Secretary James Callaghan 'having great difficulty with the Drugs Bill, where he is trying to get a different mixture of legislation, with heavier penalties for trafficking and lighter penalties for mere possession, and this has been interpreted by the newspapers as seeking concessions for pot smokers.'[56] After 'an absolutely outrageous press leak saying that... the Government was about to go soft on drugs', Callaghan returned to cabinet with a proposal not to reduce the penalties on cannabis after all. 'It became absolutely clear that the issue was really whether we should kowtow to public opinion or not,' Crossman recorded. 'Every member of the Cabinet who had been at university voted one way and everyone else voted the other... The antis, saying public opinion was too strong for us, were... outvoted... Having lost this battle, however, Callaghan whipped in with another suggestion and we did in fact give him the major concession that we would make the maximum penalty for cannabis offences not the three years originally proposed but five. The discussion was particularly fascinating because no one really doubted the rightness of the tripartite classification of drugs, the reduction of the penalties for possession and the creation of a new crime of trafficking... they simply said that the public wouldn't understand it and that we couldn't afford to alienate people on this issue.'[57]

Callaghan's bill discriminated between hard and soft drugs and, for the first time in British law, between trafficking and possession. It categorised drugs in three groups. Class A included heroin, opium, morphine, pethadine, LSD and injectable amphetamines. Class B included cannabis, various other amphetamines and drinamyl. Class C comprised amphetamines reckoned to be less dangerous. This bill eventually became the 1971 Misuse of Drugs Act. Maximum penalties for possession derive from this period. In 2000, on indictment, the maximum penalty for possession of Class A substances is seven years or an unlimited fine or both; for Class B, five years or an unlimited fine or both; for Class C, two years or an unlimited fine or both.

But these impressive provisions have failed to translate into practice. While politicians have shied away of seeming 'soft on drugs', the police and courts have exercised discretion. The result is an increasing discrepency between the severe maximum penalties concocted on public-relations grounds and the actual penalties meted out in individual cases. Of all the people dealt with for drugs possession offences in 1997, 54 per cent were cautioned, and only 11 per cent of those convicted by the courts were sentenced to custody. The 1971 Act is now largely a dead letter.

A pragmatic conclusion

British drug law has been framed not on the basis of reasoned argument or expert opinion, but in response to international and popular pressure. It has been poorly considered and hastily debated. In many instances, legislators have actually over-ridden the expert opinion of the day. The evidence suggesting that cannabis has no serious ill effects, and may even have medical benefits, has been persistently ignored. As a result of these distorting pressures, British drug legislation is full of anomalies and irrationalities. It poorly answers the needs of the British population. It is time to rethink.

The global crusade against drugs has been inspired from the outset by the United States. It has embodied the moral zeal characteristic of American political life. The first step for those who wish to improve British drug laws should be to distance themselves from these influences Instead of asking what we can learn from American experience – the question posed during the sixties with reference to marijuana and LSD, or during the false scare over crack cocaine in 1987-90 – the question should be: what, regardless of Washington, would best fulfil British interests? America has both the most punitive drug regime and the severest drug problem in the Western world. The pragmatic scepticism characteristic of Dutch policy has resulted in the lowest rate of drug-related deaths in Europe. British interests would best be fulfilled by adopting the most constructive policies found on the European mainland, and by distancing ourselves from the more dogmatic interventions of Washington. Overall, the European Union should review the effectiveness of its internal drugs laws and regulations on the understanding that neither Drug Enforcement Agency policy nor the Single Convention on Narcotic Drugs of 1961 is sacrosanct.

Not only should our legislators distance themselves from international pressures; they should also distance themselves from the domestic pressures that have weighed on them since the sixties. The medical effects of different drugs and the economic effects of prohibition are both highly technical subjects. In ignoring expert opinion in favour of popular prejudice – Callaghan's dismissal of the Wootton Report and Jack Straw's dismissal of the Runciman Report being two salient examples – our politicians have behaved unconscionably. However, there are signs that they may now be behaving foolishly as well. Callaghan's rejection of the Wootton Report was largely supported by the press; Straw's rejection of the Runciman Report was questioned by even the most conservative newspapers. The sixties generation has come of age; the moral consensus of the last forty years seems to be unravelling. The time is ripe for reform, although it will take a brave Home Secretary to admit it.

2. SOFT DRUGS AND PATERNALISM

EDWARD SKIDELSKY

One of the most striking features of the current debate on drugs in Britain is the ubiquity of paternalism. It is an attitude that unites the various sides in the debate, whatever else their differences. *Tackling Drugs to Build a Better Britain*, the government document that lays the foundation of current drugs policy, is straightforwardly paternalistic. 'Our new vision is to create a healthy and confident society, increasingly free from the harm caused by the misuse of drugs.... All drugs are harmful and enforcement against all illegal substances will continue.'[58] The government, in other words, considers itself competent to judge the harm caused by drugs and to make this judgement binding on the population as a whole. It knows my interests better than I myself, and legislates on the basis of this superior knowledge. This is the classic definition of paternalism.

Critics of the current law largely accept these paternalistic assumptions. The influential Runciman Report is a case in point. The report agrees with the government about the purpose of drug law. 'The main aim of the law must be to control and limit the demand for and the supply of illicit drugs in order to minimise the serious individual and social harms caused by their use.'[59] The report's disagreement with the government is factual rather than philosophical. It argues that cannabis causes less harm than was previously believed, and should accordingly be reclassified as a Class C drug. But the report does not challenge the exclusive right of the government to decide for the public at large which drugs are and which are not harmful. It raises no objection to paternalism.

Even those who support complete legalisation tend to share the paternalistic assumption that drug use is objectively harmful. Their opposition to prohibition is based simply on the empirical claim that prohibition compounds rather than diminishes this harm. 'Proponents of drug legalisation know the danger of drug use and wish to reduce it,' writes Richard Stevenson. 'It would be better if everyone could cope without mind-altering drugs, but prohibition is unenforceable. If some people insist on using drugs, it is better that they should buy them from law-abiding businessmen rather than criminals, and better still if they can be integrated into society and brought under medical supervision if it is needed.'[60]

Thus all three documents share the belief that taking drugs is 'harmful' or 'dangerous' and that the purpose of policy is to reduce this harm. They all exhibit what might be called 'moral' paternalism; Stevenson's essay differs from the other two only to the extent that he does not wish to translate this moral paternalism into legal paternalism. We are so accustomed to this attitude that we are in danger of forgetting how odd it is. Let us imagine for a moment that the debate is not about drugs but about religion. Suppose our government were to pronounce the practice of Islam 'harmful' and outlaw it. Suppose furthermore that opponents of religious persecution were to agree with the government that Islam is indeed harmful, disagreeing merely on the factual question of whether or not persecution augments the harm. This is not, of course, the way a liberal society treats the question of religious freedom. But it is the way we treat the question of drugs.

Some definitions
In this essay I will argue that there are no good paternalistic reasons (and no good non-paternalistic reasons) for outlawing soft drugs. But first let me introduce some definitions. It is customary to distinguish weak from strong paternalism. Weak paternalism protects an individual from harms that he himself would recognise as such were he properly informed. If I forcibly prevent you crossing a bridge that I happen to know is unsafe, then I am engaging in weak paternalism. Strong paternalism protects against harms that even a perfectly informed individual might not acknowledge as such. It rests upon a notion of 'objective harm' – harm that is entirely independent of individual apprehension. Strong paternalism is a species of what is sometimes called 'legal moralism'. I will argue that whereas weak paternalism is a legitimate basis of legislation in a liberal society, strong paternalism – except in a very few exceptional cases – is not. Yet our laws against soft drugs are an example of strong, not weak paternalism.

By 'soft drugs' I mean drugs that are not both highly addictive and debilitating. (Coffee and cigarettes are highly addictive but not debilitating; LSD is debilitating if taken frequently but is not addictive; these all therefore count as soft drugs.) Whether a particular drug is soft or hard is a delicate empirical question. It is quite possible that none of the drugs currently on offer are hard in my sense. The addictiveness of both heroin and cocaine is greatly over-estimated. Some studies show that at any given time only 10 percent of heroin and cocaine users can be classified as addicts, which is roughly the same

as the percentage of drinkers who can be classified as alcoholics.[61] The degree
to which heroin and cocaine are debilitating is also in dispute. According to the
U.S. Department of Labor, 77 percent of 'serious cocaine users' are in regular
employment.[62] Were cocaine legal, the figure would no doubt be even higher.
But I want to leave heroin and cocaine to one side, because the data on them
is sketchy and disputed. What is beyond doubt is that cannabis, LSD and
Ecstasy are all soft in the sense defined above. Current medical opinion rates all
of them as less addictive than alcohol and tobacco.[63] They should all, if my
argument is sound, be legalised.

Why do I not include hard drugs in my argument? The answer is that hard
drugs constitute one of those exceptional cases in which strong paternalism is
arguably legitimate. Addiction to hard drugs involves a loss of freedom. And
loss of freedom is the only harm to which a liberal state attaches an objective
rather than a merely subjective meaning. Freedom is, as the saying goes,
inalienable. This is why a liberal society does not permit a person to sell himself
into slavery. To the extent that addiction to hard drugs is equivalent to selling
oneself into slavery, it is similarly impermissible. Hard drugs are one sphere in
which strong paternalism may be legitimate. Whether or not it is enforceable is
of course another matter.[64]

The decay of paternalism

That 'harmful' and 'beneficial' must be defined relative to the choices of the
individual strikes us today as patently true. If I choose to go to the cinema of
an evening, who has the right to tell me that I am harming myself? What I
choose to do is, by definition, what is good for me. This subjective conception
of the good is the intellectual foundation of the free market economy. It is
because interests are revealed only in choice ('revealed preference') that a
system of free association is required to guarantee their satisfaction. If the
interests of an individual could be specified in advance, prior to his choosing
any one thing over another, then there could be no objection to a central
allocation of goods.

So ubiquitous is this subjective conception of good that we sometimes
forget that it is the product of a specific historical evolution. The ancient
Greeks held a strictly objective view of the good. For Plato, harms and benefits
to the soul are as palpable as harms and benefits to the body and as little
dependent on personal preference. For Aristotle, likewise, an individual's ends
are inherent in his nature as a rational animal and depend not a whit on his

own choices. Both Plato and Aristotle were – logically, given their premises – paternalists; both believed in rule by an enlightened elite. This objective conception of the good passed into Christian orthodoxy. What is good, for the Christian, depends not on individual choice but on the will of God. This explains the vehemence of the wars of religion. The perpetrators of these wars were highly principled paternalists. They were sincerely trying to save their enemies from a harm – eternal damnation – arising from their own free choice.

The rise of modern subjectivism is a story that can be told in many ways. The decline of organised religion, with its various prohibitions on the expression of private desire, is clearly fundamental. The growth of the market economy, and the legitimisation of individual choice that it entailed, is another aspect of the same process. But the story also has a purely intellectual dimension. The central episode here is the development of German romanticism at the end of the eighteenth century. The German romantics seized upon the old truism that all individuals are different and invested it with a new significance. Prior to this point, differences between individuals had been interpreted merely as differences of taste and aptitude. These differences were in no way held to qualify the universality of our moral and intellectual standards. The romantics interpreted human difference in a much more radical fashion. Each human being harbours his own unique *genius*, his inward pattern of development. There is no longer any one measure of human excellence, any one prototype to which we must all conform. 'Every human being has his own measure,' wrote Herder, 'an accord, peculiar to him, of all his feelings to one another.'[65]

The idea that every individual carries within him his own standard of value was to find its fullest expression in the literature and art of the nineteenth century. The novel, in particular, was to become the medium for investigating this deepened sense of individuality. 'Souls have complexions too,' says George Eliot's Dorothea, 'What will suit one will not suit another.' Celia is attracted by jewellery and the affable Sir George; Dorothea by austerity and the grave Casaubon. Neither is right nor wrong; they are just different.

The romantic emphasis on self-expression was not only influential in literature; it was also to have an important impact on the development of political liberalism. It forms the basis of Humboldt's essay, *The Limits of State Action*, written in 1791-2. 'Whatever does not spring from a man's free choice,' writes Humboldt, 'does not enter into his very being, but still remains alien to his true nature; he does not perform it with truly human energies, but merely with mechanical exactness.'[66] The morality of an act does not lie in its conformity to an external standard, but in the quality of motive underlying it. A good action performed in obedience to the law, or out of fear of public disapproval, is not truly good. Humboldt draws the conclusion that 'any state interference in private affairs, where there is no immediate reference to violence done to individual rights, should be absolutely condemned.'[67]

The Limits of State Action is known in England chiefly for its influence on John Stuart Mill. Humboldt's conception of human freedom forms the basis of the famous argument in chapter III of *On Liberty*. 'Human nature is not a machine to be built after a model, and set to do exactly the work prescribed for it, but a tree, which requires to grow and develop itself on all sides, according to the tendencies of the inward forces which make it a living thing.'[68] We must therefore, argues Mill, grant to each individual the greatest possible freedom to follow unhindered the natural bent of his personality. This freedom must be vigilantly defended against both government action and public opinion. Otherwise our natural human capacities will become 'withered and starved'.[69]

As far as the regulation of religion and sexual morality is concerned, the twentieth century has fulfilled, and even surpassed, the vision of Humboldt and Mill. Practices that were previously condemned, both by law and public opinion, as heretical or perverse are now viewed as unobjectionable manifestations of private choice. The language in which this development is justified still recalls, in a truncated and stilted fashion, that of romanticism. Sexual and religious practices are no longer judged according to an objective norm, but are seen as 'expressions' of 'personality' or of 'culture'. The very notion of an objective norm in these spheres has largely broken down. Choice has become the arbiter of the good. It is the fact that I choose *x* that makes it good for me, not the fact that *x* is good that makes it right for me to choose it.

Religious believers hold fast to the idea of an objective moral order. Within the framework of such an order, paternalism still makes sense. But the notion of an 'objective moral order' has undergone a profound shrinkage. To the medieval Christian, the moral order of the universe was something public, something almost tangible. Dante could talk about 'the love that moves the sun and other stars'. To us, this statement is comprehensible only as a poetic metaphor. God is no longer manifest in the movement of the heavens. He has been reduced to an object of private devotion. This severely limits the scope of religious paternalism. The individual believer can still choose to submit to religious authority, but this act of submission nonetheless derives its legitimacy from the fact that it is *his choice*. Joining a church, like joining the army, is a voluntary and rescindable surrender of freedom. Once again, choice is the ultimate arbiter of the good. No religious authority is entitled to impose its prescriptions without consent, because the metaphysical certainties that would once have justified such an imposition have long been destroyed.

The upshot of these developments is that strong paternalism has largely lost its meaning. It makes no sense for the state to circumscribe my choices 'for my own good' if 'my own good' can be defined only as what I choose. This is the source of the familiar liberal demand that the state remain neutral between rival conceptions of the good. It is not merely that the state has no superior knowledge of the good, or that it lacks the means to enforce the good; it is that there is no such thing as 'the good' to be known or enforced. Strong paternalism, in most areas, is not so much wrong as meaningless.

Paternalist arguments for soft drug prohibition

Yet there is one important area of legislation that has not only escaped, but actually contradicted the development outlined above. This is the burgeoning field of 'health and safety' legislation. Why this should be so is an extremely interesting question. The need to prevent people from 'free-riding' on a nationalised health service is clearly part of the answer, but it cannot be the whole answer. The law against driving without a seatbelt actually imposes extra costs on the NHS, for victims of accidents are now merely injured who would previously have been killed. More important is the fact that health and safety legislation, unlike moral and religious legislation, can claim the authority of science. Physical health, unlike moral well-being, is not considered a matter of private opinion. It can be measured scientifically. A liberal state can therefore take a stance on matters of public health without appearing to compromise its neutrality. Harms to the soul are left to conscience to decide; harms to the body are a fit object of official adjudication.

Not only is health measurable; it is also patently a good thing. No rational person would prefer, other things being equal, sickness over health. Health and safety legislation thus appears to be an example of *weak as* opposed to *strong* paternalism; it protects us against harms that we already acknowledge as such. Take the law against selling lawnmowers without safety guards. The harm that this law protects us from is one that any rational and well-informed individual might be expected to recognise. The law merely centralises, in a maximally efficient way, the costs of information gathering. We do not all have the time or expertise to assess the risks of using an unprotected lawnmower, so the state saves us the trouble by making the assessment for us. In doing this, it does not impose on us any ends that we do not already implicitly accept. That is why health and safety legislation is not, for the most part, experienced as a grievous deprivation of liberty.

Yet not all health and safety legislation falls so innocuously into the category of weak paternalism. A law is only weakly paternalistic if the harm that it protects us from is not accompanied by any benefits. (Using a lawnmower without a safety guard entails no benefits; to ban such lawnmowers is therefore weak paternalism.) But the moment the harm in question is accompanied by benefits, paternalism becomes more problematic. For it now involves the judgement not merely that the activity in question is harmful, but also that this harm *outweighs* the accompanying benefits. And this second judgement is not one to which any rational and well-informed person can automatically be assumed to consent. It is a judgement of value, not a judgement of fact. Weak paternalism has become strong paternalism.

Take, for example, the stringent hygiene directives issued by the European Commission. These enforce a much higher standard of hygiene than many people deem necessary, at considerable cost to both consumer and producer. Or take the seatbelt law. Driving a car without a seatbelt, unlike using a lawnmower without a safety guard, is regarded by some people as dashingly reckless. It carries benefits. By making it illegal, the state is in effect claiming that these benefits are unworthy of consideration. Both the European hygiene directives and the seatbelt law contain an implicit moral judgement. They assert that we *should* be more concerned about our health or our safety than we in fact are. They impose on us a hierarchy of values that is not necessarily our own. And yet they are hardly ever explicitly justified in such terms. The language of health and safety endows pure legal moralism with the appearance of neutrality.

The law against drugs is increasingly presented as a piece of health and safety legislation. In the words of the government document quoted above, 'all drugs are harmful and enforcement against all illegal substances will continue.'[70] In a parliamentary debate on the 12th April 2000, Home Office minister Charles Clarke defended the law against cannabis on grounds of health. 'The chronic effects include damage to mental functioning, especially learning abilities, which may not be reversible for prolonged and heavy users....

and the drug can exacerbate schizophrenia in people who are already affected by that illness. There are also obvious health risks associated with smoking the drug.'[71] The prohibition of Ecstasy is constantly defended on the basis of its (much exaggerated) risks. The Labour government is clearly anxious to avoid presenting its campaign against drugs as an ethical crusade, and so has shifted the debate onto the more neutral terrain of health and safety.

But how successful is this manoeuvre? As I have argued above, a health and safety law only qualifies as weakly paternalistic if the danger that it protects us from is not accompanied by any benefits. Only then can it be claimed that the law furthers ends that any rational and informed person would endorse. Is this true of the law against drugs? Quite evidently it is not. Drugs carry benefits, in the eyes of those who use them, that adequately compensate for the risks. These compensatory benefits don't have to be conceived in intellectual or mystical terms; pleasure is itself a benefit. Indeed, the mere fact that people *choose* to take drugs shows that they benefit them. In refusing to take these benefits into consideration, the government is implying that they are in some sense *unworthy* of consideration, that they are perverted or illusory. And this is the expression of a moral stance, not a statement of scientific fact. The state does not prohibit (say) mountain climbing, which is statistically far more dangerous than taking drugs. The reason for this discrepancy can only be that mountain climbing is presumed to have some sort of invigorating effect upon the character – which might, in the opinion of some, compensate for its dangers – whereas drug taking is not.

Thus the seemingly neutral, medical justification for the ban on soft drugs turns out, on closer inspection, to rest upon moral disapproval. What is strange is that the same disapproval is shared by many legalisers. It is considered almost obligatory, among advocates of legalisation, to declare that one sees no good in taking drugs. 'It would be better if everyone could cope without mind-altering drugs,' writes Richard Stevenson in the passage quoted above, 'but prohibition is unenforceable.'[72] John Kaplan, the well-known advocate of cannabis legalisation, expresses similar thoughts. 'I cannot escape the feeling that drug use, aside from any harm it does, is somehow wrong.'[73] Advocates of legalisation obviously feel a need to affirm their respectability, to distance themselves from 'the hippies'. Perhaps they consider such an affirmation necessary in order to gain a respectful hearing. But it concedes far too much to the opposition. If soft drug use really did constitute an objective moral harm, as Stevenson and Kaplan suggest, then a policy of paternalism would be meaningful even if unenforceable. But if it does not constitute an objective moral harm, as I have argued, then a policy of paternalism suffers from the more fundamental defect of being meaningless. It is time that legalisers overcame their deference to respectable opinion and admitted that taking drugs can be fun.

I have suggested that the familiar argument for prohibition on grounds of health ultimately rests upon moral disapproval. But is this necessarily an objection to it? Our statute books contain other laws based on nothing stronger than moral disapproval. These include the laws against bestiality, necrophilia and incest. None of these laws is defensible from a liberal point of view, and yet there is no great clamour for their repeal. This is because they rest upon a primordial taboo, on a feeling that the behaviour in question is beyond the pale. Perhaps our law against drugs rests upon a similar taboo? If it does, then objections of the kind that I have been raising simply miss the point.

Certain facts support this interpretation. The intense, irrational horror that drugs arouse in many people does indeed suggest the operation of a taboo. Anti-drug crusaders, particularly in America, do not hide the fact that they think drugs evil. 'I find no merit in the legalizers case,' writes the former American drug tsar William Bennett. 'The simple fact is that drug use is wrong. And the moral argument, in the end, is the most compelling argument.'[74] Most American states have laws against the public sale of drug paraphernalia. Since, as James Bakalar and Lester Grinspoon point out, there is no evidence that these laws have any effect on consumption, they can only be explained as an expression of moral disapproval.[75] Drug paraphernalia, like pornography, is deemed an 'offence against decency' that must be hidden from the public eye.

But although moral disapproval is clearly an important *motivation* for the war against drugs, it doesn't – in this country at any rate – feature in its official *justification*. The publications of the current government scrupulously avoid all talk of good and evil, focussing instead on the damage wrought by drugs to health. There is a good reason for this. The taboos against incest, necrophilia and bestiality have deep roots in European history. They may even have a biological basis. There is no clamour for the legalisation of these acts, presumably because no one wants to be suspected of actually practicing them. The taboo against drugs, by contrast, has no deep cultural or biological roots. It is a product of recent history, and is rejected by a large part of the population. There is even less justification for enshrining it in law than there is for enshrining the still widespread disapproval of homosexuality in law. If it is indeed true that our law against soft drugs rests upon hidden moral disapproval, then that is *ipso facto* a reason for rejecting it.

Non-paternalist arguments for soft drug prohibition

Occasionally the paternalist arguments outlined above are supplemented with non-paternalist arguments. Soft drugs should remain illegal, it is argued, not because they harm the user but because they harm others. The most common version of this argument invokes the free-rider dilemma. It seems unfair that regular soft drug users, whose health problems are largely self-inflicted, should benefit from free provision on the National Health Service to the same degree as everyone else. This is true, but to pass directly from this premise to the conclusion that soft drugs should be illegal is a staggering *non sequitur*. The criminal law is surely not the correct instrument to handle what is essentially a problem of insurance. The difficulty might be dealt with easily by imposing a tax on soft drugs to cover the extra burden on the NHS. This device works smoothly in the case of tobacco and alcohol. There is no need to infringe on private liberties. The fact that the government feels justified in infringing on private liberties in its campaign against drugs suggests that more than mere externalities are at stake.

The other non-paternalist argument commonly heard rests on an analogy between drug use and infectious disease. The soft drug user, it is said, harms not only himself but all those he 'infects' with the bacillus of drug use. State measures are required to prevent harm to these innocent third parties, just as they are required to prevent the spread of plague. William Bennett urges that casual drug users be punished especially severely, because 'a non-addict's drug use... is *highly* contagious.'[76] The frequent use, in the press and in academic literature, of the term 'epidemic' to refer to outbreaks of drug use reinforces the analogy. But it is nonetheless spurious. It obscures the crucial distinction between voluntary action and involuntary effect. People are not 'infected' with drug use; they *choose* to use drugs. The analogy with infectious disease only becomes plausible on the assumption – again, a moralistic assumption – that drugs are so patently bad that no rational person would choose to take them. All kinds of pseudo-concepts, such as 'infection' or 'peer group pressure', are then invoked to explain why people do in fact take drugs. Yet the reason people take drugs is very simple: they enjoy it. Nothing more needs to be said on the subject.

These two non-paternalist arguments will only appear remotely valid to those predisposed, on other grounds, to scorn the use of drugs. Like the paternalist argument examined above, they are *post hoc* rationalisations of what is essentially an ethical position. However much the government tries to state its case in the sanitised language of public health and economics, it cannot escape the charge of Puritanism.

Conclusion

Such philosophical considerations are all very well, it will be said, but what actually follows from them? Issues of abstract right pale in significance before the practical problems of legalisation. The government is constrained by international treatise obligations; it must consider the effects of legalisation on minors and the mentally unstable; it must decide what sort of constraints to put on the sale and advertisement of drugs; it must decide whether and at what level to tax them. All these are, of course, serious problems. It does not follow from anything I have said that soft drugs should be legalised overnight. But we must be clear about the general direction we wish drug policy to take. It is only once the general direction of policy has been determined that the individual details come into focus. The first question to be asked of any law is: is it just? If we decide that it is unjust, we have made a commitment to overcome any practical difficulties that might stand in the way of reform.

PART II
The Problem of Addiction

3. ADDICTION AND FREE WILL

Diana Gardner

> ... at the time I began to take opium daily, I could not have done otherwise.
> Whether indeed, afterwards I might not have succeeded in breaking
> off the habit, even when it seemed to me that all efforts would be
> unavailing, and whether many of the innumerable efforts which I did
> make might not have been carried much further, and my gradual
> re-conquests of ground lost might not have been followed up much more
> energetically – these are questions which I must decline.

> Thomas De Quincey,
> Confessions of an English Opium Eater 1821

Opponents of the current law against drugs often accuse its defenders of infringing upon individual freedom. A liberal state, they argue, should observe John Stuart Mill's principle of not prohibiting actions that do not harm others. But even many defenders of individual liberty recognise exceptions to Mill's principle. They permit state intervention in those rare cases where it is necessary to preserve an individual's freedom. It is often argued that the use of addictive drugs is one such case. Addiction, it is said, robs the addict of her free will: she cannot help but take a particular drug when that drug is available to her. Thus the prohibition of drug use actually protects individual freedom rather than violating it.

But what exactly is this curious phenomenon called addiction? When addicts say they want a certain outcome but act in ways that make that outcome impossible, are they just particularly convincing liars, are they egregiously fickle, or are they really in the grip of something that obliterates any ability to choose? Much of the philosophical literature on personal autonomy tends to assume the latter. Robert Goodin, for example, compares the addict with the person who has been 'physically restrained, in a way that rendered him simply unable to do what he said he wanted to do.'[77] The melodramatic portrayal of addiction in the cinema and the press tends to reinforce this stereotype.

I will argue that it is a mistake to conceive of addiction as binding a person in this way. For one thing, it cannot explain the fact that many former addicts have managed to overcome their addictions. Addiction may, it is true, render a person *less* free to exercise her will as she pleases. Other distractions and temptations clamour for her attention; these present obstacles that she would not have to overcome had she not become addicted in the first place. Thus addiction does compromise personal autonomy. But then so do many other habits and needs. The question must be whether addiction compromises personal autonomy to such an extent as to warrant intervention by the state. After providing a brief overview of the nature of autonomy, I will consider the ways in which chronic drug-use creates hurdles for the addict who wants to abstain. I will argue that none of them impede the addict's ability to lead her life to such an extent that the current law on drugs is justified on the grounds that it 'protects her freedom'.

Autonomy
In the philosophical discussion of free will, a distinction is often made between higher- and lower-order desires. Lower-order desires are the ordinary desires that we have for things, people and states-of-affairs. Higher-order desires are desires that have lower-order desires as their object; they are, in other words, desires to have or not to have other desires.[78] Higher-order desires typically relate to the kind of life I want to lead or to the kind of person that I want to be. For example, I might have a lower-order desire to comfort an injured dog I find on the side of the road. After some critical reflection, I endorse this desire because I believe that people should show compassion to other sentient beings (or simply because I want to be the sort of person who is moved by compassion[79]). Here, my higher-order desire (to treat animals with compassion) is congruent with my lower-order desire (to tend to this dog). My lower-order desire moves me to act in a way that is consistent with the kind of person I have a higher-order desire to be.

Higher- and lower-order desires don't always mesh so easily, however. A vegetarian may have a higher-order desire not to want to eat meat, but nonetheless be unable to resist her lower-order desire for roast lamb. Scenarios such as these, in which we follow our lower-order desires against our higher order desires, are what we customarily call a lapse of free will.

But the occasional lapse of free will is not an abdication of autonomy. Autonomy is a 'global' rather than a 'local' concept. Calling a person autonomous requires us to make a judgement about how she conducts herself over the course of her whole life. If a person is generally self-directing, or has not abdicated overall responsibility for how her life turns out, then it is correct to describe her as autonomous even if she has occasional lapses of free will.[80] Thus the would-be vegetarian who only occasionally yields to the temptation of roast lamb can still be regarded as an autonomous agent. But if the would-be vegetarian regularly eats meat, we have cause to doubt either her commitment to her professed higher-order desire or her competence to realise that desire. If her commitment is real but her competence lacking, then we can say that her free will has been significantly undermined.

Addiction

Addiction is often assimilated to this last scenario. The case we are all familiar with is that of the smoker who continually yields to the temptation of a cigarette even though she professes a desire to quit smoking. Her lower-order desire to smoke appears to have over-whelmed her higher-order desire not to want to smoke. The question we have to consider is whether such inconsistency constitutes a total abnegation of autonomy, or only a qualification of it.

Definitions of addiction are as numerous and various as the agendas of those who proffer them.[81] While some experts hold that addiction is both physiological and psychological, others insist that it is predominantly or solely psychological and others that it is physiological only.[82] There exists a strong temptation to ground explanations of addition in the physiological. As Philip Bean observes, 'once the definition [of addiction] is allowed to slip its physiological anchor, it allows greater levels of moral evaluations to be included, and hence greater opportunities for controlling such activities as are seen as unworthy or merely disliked.'[83] However, this insistence that 'addiction' remain rigidly fastened in the physiological is somewhat arbitrary. It might draw a clear line, but it does not tell us why that line has been drawn where it has or how we should regard activities on either side of it.

Despite disagreement over definitions, descriptions of certain phenomena tend to recur throughout the literature on addiction. Included among these are withdrawal, relapse, 'crowding out', chronic (or long-term) administration, tolerance, craving, compulsive use and ambivalence. Rather than adopt a single definition of addiction here, I will consider these various features of drug dependency in turn. I will discuss whether, and to what extent, they compromise the personal autonomy of the addict.

Physical withdrawal and conditioned behaviour
One well-known feature of drug addiction is the withdrawal symptoms that

addicts suffer when they abstain after prolonged use. The severity of these symptoms varies widely from drug to drug, from irritability and mild headaches after giving up caffeine, anxiety and (sometimes) tremors after giving up alcohol, to stomach cramps, diarrhoea and tremors after giving up opiates. Other drugs, such as LSD, appear not to produce withdrawal symptoms at all.

Withdrawal symptoms seem to compromise personal autonomy in a number of ways. The most obvious is that the desire to avoid discomfort and pain leads a person to take a further dose of the drug, even though she has a higher-order desire to cease using that drug. Psychological research also suggests that withdrawal may operate in more subtle ways to increase the desire for drugs. For instance, individuals may learn to perform acts – such as further drug-taking – that alleviate unpleasant withdrawal symptoms. They gradually come to associate taking the drug with the relief that alleviation of withdrawal brings. Thus further drug use not only alleviates the physical unpleasantness of sudden abstention, but also works – by a process of Pavlovian-style conditioning – to 'reinforce' the appetite for continued use.[84] Withdrawal, then, may plausibly be said to bolster an addict's desire to continue to use drugs.

But does it deprive the addict of personal autonomy? The mere wish to avoid the physical discomfort of withdrawal is clearly not sufficient to deprive the addict of all control over whether or not she takes more drugs. If the desire to avoid of pain or discomfort were overwhelming, then I would have *no choice* but to avoid visits to the dentist. Addicts often endure successfully the pains of physical withdrawal (on their own or in detox clinics), a fact that is inexplicable on the assumption that the fear of withdrawal has deprived them of their autonomy.

The conditioned behaviour arising from the relief of withdrawal symptoms seems to provide a stronger reason for supposing that an addict's personal autonomy has been destroyed, since it is subtler and the addict may not always be aware of it. But this conclusion is not in fact warranted. So long as individuals are able to recognise a particular behaviour as incompatible with their conception of the kind of person they want to be, and are able to take measures to change it, the tyranny of conditioned behaviour can be overcome. A shy or self-effacing person may take an assertiveness training course; a 'hot-head' may take an anger-management course. Similarly, an addict can attend a drug-rehabilitation course or attend a self-help group such as Narcotics Anonymous or Alcoholics

Anonymous. Conditioned behaviour is an impediment to changing one's way of life, but not an insurmountable one.

'Crowding-out' or 'salience'

Another phenomenon commonly associated with addiction is known in the literature as 'crowding-out' or 'salience'. This refers to the dominance of drugs in the addict's life. For many addicts, drug-use assumes an increasingly overwhelming priority; it leads them to shed other interests they may once have had.

But crowding-out is not a necessary condition of drug addiction. Nicotine- and caffeine-addiction constitute obvious counter-examples to the salience thesis. It is unknown to hear of a caffeine-addict giving up a hobby because she is now too busy drinking coffee, or of a smoker giving up work because she wants to stay home and smoke. But that does not give us reason to suppose that smokers and coffee-drinkers are any less addicted to nicotine or caffeine.

Neither is crowding out peculiar to drug addiction. Monomaniacal behaviour can also be observed in cases of religious devotion and romantic attachment. Famous novels, as well as daily newspapers, frequently recount episodes in which individuals have allowed religious zeal or romantic fervour to overrun their lives.

It might be replied that 'crowding out' is the exception rather than the rule in these cases, but there is no reason to suppose that this is not also true of drug dependency. Numerous alcoholics, for example, pursue careers and maintain relationships while continuing to drink. Many recreational users of drugs (including a significant number who would experience physical withdrawal upon cessation) do not allow the drug to inhabit a position of excessive prominence in their lives. This percentage would no doubt be higher were drugs more easily available. In Switzerland, where heroin was legally dispensed to some addicts between 1994 and 1996, many were able to prevent addiction from crowding out other activities. Addicts who had previously been homeless and unemployed, stealing to finance their addiction, were reported as holding down steady jobs and maintaining stable homes.[85] Most opiate addicts in the nineteenth century were able to lead stable, productive lives. The suspicion must be that crowding out is less a function of heroin addiction as such than of its illegality.

Even if obsession were a defining feature of drug addiction, this would not in itself give us grounds for legislation. We might agree that a life devoted entirely to drugs is not the best life to live, just as we think that the 'workaholic' misses out on other valuable experiences by devoting all her energies to work. But we do not think that the state ought to prohibit lifestyles that are regarded as unorthodox by others.

Relapse and rapid reinstatement

The phenomenon of 'relapse' is also one that has been cited as evidence of the fact that drug use undermines autonomy. There are a number of psychological and neurobiological theories to explain why drug addicts often start taking drugs again, despite having survived the unpleasant withdrawal process and a period of abstinence. The feelings of shame and guilt that work to sustain alcoholism, gambling problems, compulsive shopping and overeating[86] may also be implicated in 'relapse and reinstatement'. Following a minor lapse, the reformer may cope with her feelings of guilt by returning to her old 'coping' behaviour -drinking, smoking or over-eating. There are other ways in which abstinence violation can lead to a resumption of the addictive behaviour. One or two minor lapses may lead the addict to deny that she was ever seriously trying to abstain, because she doesn't want to admit that she has failed.[87] Or else it may lead her to believe that she is hopelessly addicted, because this gives her an excuse to abandon the struggle.[88]

Another theory of addiction holds that relapse is caused by cue-conditioned craving. According to George Loewenstein, 'relapse is a constant threat because craving can be initiated by almost any environmental cue that becomes associated with the drug'.[89] Throughout an individual's drug-using 'career', various places and situations will come to be associated in her mind with drug use. This cue-conditioning has implications for the success of any decision she later makes to abstain. For one thing, abstention requires the addict to change her environment, either by ridding it of evocative cues or else by removing herself from it altogether. As Loewenstein observes, 'Successful quitting is likely to require a substantial investment in change of environment and lifestyle'.[90] The addict can also try to defuse the cues themselves, by changing the behaviour she associates with them. This also requires considerable effort. But having made this investment in changing her environment (or her visceral responses to it), the addict still has no guarantee that she will be protected against cue-conditioned craving. She may not be aware of all the places and situations associated in her mind with her former drug use, and so will not be able to avoid or eradicate everything that might induce craving. Suggestive cues can appear unexpectedly, so the abstinent addict has little opportunity to brace herself for the craving that she is about to experience.

Neurochemical theories of addiction assert that chronic drug use permanently affects the release and reuptake of the neurone dopamine in the reward pathways of the brain, rendering the addict continually vulnerable to relapse.[91] The various addictive drugs affect dopaminergic functioning differently. Cocaine eliminates the uptake of dopamine by neurons and so causes it to become concentrated in the synapses;[92] opiates, on the other hand, work by releasing dopamine directly into the reward pathways.[93] Nevertheless, most addictive drugs appear to stimulate the dopamine system in one way or another.

According to Eliot L. Gardner and James David,[94] relapse can be triggered by small 'priming' doses of drugs that increase dopaminergic functioning in the brain's reward centres. The priming dose does not have to be of the same drug that the individual was formerly addicted to; laboratory research suggests that 'cross-priming' can occur. For instance, 'priming doses of morphine reinstate cocaine self-administration and priming doses of amphetamine or of the dopaminergic agonist bromocriptine reinstate heroin-trained responding.'[95]

Gardner and David conclude that chronic drug use has three effects. It permanently alters the pleasure/reward circuitry in the drug-user's brain, increasing her vulnerability to re-addiction. It creates a vulnerability to other drugs that stimulate the brain's reward system, even drugs that the user has no previous experience of. And it renders the addict vulnerable to internal and external cues associated with her former drug taking.[96] Gardner and David describe these effects as 'a series of virtually insurmountable neurobiological hurdles... erected in the path of drug addicts wishing to stay abstinent.'[97] If this is true, then drug addiction clearly undermines personal autonomy. The addict who wishes to come clean has to contend with 'virtually insurmountable' neurobiological obstacles. Her higher-order desire for abstinence is impotent in the face of her chemically driven lower-order desire for the drug.

But do these neurobiological changes really create an *insurmountable* obstacle to the exercise of autonomy? Human beings are not, after all, hostages to the passions that afflict them. Unlike animals, they can study and control their desires. This capacity for reflection and self-control is the essence of human freedom. A former drug addict can employ a number of strategies to help her to avoid a return to the lifestyle she now rejects. She can, as has already been mentioned, try to stay away from or defuse cues. Where conditioned cues cannot be avoided or defused, there remain a number of techniques for enduring the ensuing craving.[98]

It is also important to bear in mind that occasional lapses do not rob a person of autonomy. Autonomy, as has been mentioned, is a global concept; it is the ability to direct the general course of one's life, rather than to exercise control over every single detail. The recovering addict who is generally abstinent but occasionally fails to resist temptation does not thereby lose her autonomy. It is only when an addict consistently violates her own resolve not to take drugs that her autonomy is called into question.

It is none the less true that drug addiction compromises autonomy in a number of ways. The former addict who wishes to remain abstinent must avoid or defuse certain cues, refrain from taking the drug to which she was formerly addicted and eschew certain other drugs as well.[99] This limits the abstinent addict's freedom of action. A heroin addict who wants to come clean no longer has the option of taking amphetamines.[100] Had she not become addicted to heroin in the first place, amphetamines would still be available to her. Still, this limiting of options hardly constitutes a complete loss of autonomy. It simply means that the former addict must exercise a level of caution with regard to drugs that the non-addict does not have to exercise.

Ambivalence

Nevertheless, it will be argued, there are many cases in which an addict persistently violates her own resolve not to take drugs. Her lower-order desire for the drug constantly overwhelms her higher-order desire to stay clean. Surely this is a *prima facie* example of loss of autonomy?

Cases such as these undoubtedly occur. But where the failure to give up is repeated, it can be doubted whether the professed desire to give up is sincere or unambiguous. It may be not that a higher-order desire to quit is overwhelmed by a lower-order desire for the drug, but that a higher-order desire to quit has to contend with another higher-order desire not to quit. The conflict, in short, is *between higher-order desires themselves.*[101] This is what is often known as ambivalence. Ambivalence is not the same as impaired autonomy. An ambivalent person is someone who cannot decide which of several higher-order desires to identify with, rather than someone who has decided on one or the other yet finds herself unable to act in accordance with it. An ambivalent addict wishes to be rid of the costs of addiction but to hold on to its benefits. She is not unfree; she simply cannot make up her mind.

We are thus not entitled to act on the assumption that addicts always want to give up.[102] Addiction undoubtedly carries costs, and for this reason many people think that addicts *should* want to give up. But this is an assertion about what addicts ought to desire, not about what they do in fact desire. This has an obvious bearing on the contentious question of coercive treatment. Such treatment is often justified on the grounds that it *liberates* the addict from her addiction. This assumes that the addict wants to be liberated from her addiction. But if she wants to carry on being addicted, then to force her to undergo treatment is not to liberate her; it is simply to impose on her an end that is not her own. Is a liberal state really justified in imposing its moral values on citizens in this way? Using the power of the state to enforce a particular conception of the good is precisely the kind of paternalism against which John Stuart Mill so passionately protested.

It is not obvious that coercive treatment can succeed even by its own lights. Deciding which of our many higher-order desires to identify with is something that *we do to ourselves*. Others may attempt to influence the decision (using a variety of tactics, from bullying to gentle persuasion) but the final commitment must come from the individual concerned. The conflict that needs to be resolved is an internal one; the will to resolve it must therefore come from within.[103]

Conclusion

The current law against drugs ensures that the life of a heroin or cocaine addict is usually a wretched one. High prices force her into debt and crime; poor quality black-market drugs exact a severe toll on her health. Under the Crime and Disorder Act of 1998, she may be forced to undergo coercive treatment for her addiction as an alternative to prison.[104] No other section of the population is subjected to such illiberal treatment.

This inhuman policy is justified only if drug addiction robs people of their autonomy. Liberal states reserve the right to prevent citizens from throwing away their liberty. This is why slavery contracts are not recognised in British law. If addiction could accurately be described as a form of self-imposed slavery – if it were equivalent, in the phrase of Robert Goodin, to physical restraint – then the draconian treatment of drug addicts might have some justification.

I have argued in this essay that addiction is *not* a form of self-imposed slavery. Addiction may *weaken* autonomy, by increasing the addict's vulnerability to temptation, but it is a mis-description of the phenomenon to claim that it *destroys* autonomy. The impact of addiction on free will is not as devastating as much of the literature on the subject would have one believe. We all face competing impulses, desires and temptations, whether physiological or otherwise. But they are seldom so overwhelming as to deny us all control over our entire life.

Nonetheless, addiction to heroin and cocaine does diminish autonomy to a certain degree. This is an inescapable implication of the very term 'addiction'. If 'addiction' did not entail any diminution of autonomy, then it would be an empty concept. Some extreme libertarians have indeed embraced this conclusion, urging that we do away with the whole notion of addiction.[105] This is not a view I share. Addiction is a useful and widely recognised psychological category. The fact that it cannot be given a precise physiological definition does not justify doing away with it altogether.

The fact that certain drugs are both addictive and harmful is a reason to treat them differently from ordinary goods. This is the logic behind the various restrictions on the sale and advertising of alcohol and cigarettes. A similar reasoning also applies to cocaine and heroin. Addictiveness justifies a certain degree of state intervention, but not the degree of intervention exemplified by current policy.

A middle-way is required. Without committing itself to full legalisation, the government could do much to redress the injustice currently inflicted on addicts. Two steps that might be taken immediately are the decriminalisation of possession for personal use, and the abolition of the coercive treatment prescribed by the 1998 Crime and Disorder Act. A longer-term goal should be the introduction of heroin and possibly cocaine prescription for registered addicts, together with the provision of clean needles and counselling services. Such measures lack the logical simplicity of both thoroughgoing legalisation and thoroughgoing prohibition. But they are the only way of doing justice to the peculiar status of addiction – a condition higher than total servitude, but lower than full autonomy.

4. THE VARIETIES OF ADDICTION

JAMES BAKALAR

Despite many years of bitter dispute and a century of increasingly harsh government controls, the question of how a free society should respond to drug use and abuse remains unresolved. We have to balance the requirements of health, safety, and social order against the values of individual freedom and diversity of experience. In making these decisions, we must pay special attention to addiction or dependence. It is largely (although not entirely) because of addiction that drug use has serious effects on mental and physical health, economic productivity, family life, and social order. Addiction is also the most plausible justification for saying that exposure to drugs causes a loss of personal freedom and that therefore the desire to take drugs should not be treated on a par, socially or legally, with other individual desires.[106]

But addiction proves remarkably difficult to define. As we shall see, it is a highly complex phenomenon, varying considerably from person to person. To get a better understanding of the term, it is useful to start with the American Psychiatric Association's description of addiction as a medical diagnosis – as good an attempt as any to provide an authoritative definition. It expresses an unstable mixture of biological, psychological, and social concerns. The symptoms of substance dependence (a synonym for addiction), as described in the A.P.A. diagnostic manual, fall into three classes: physiological states (tolerance and a physical withdrawal reaction); undesirable behaviour with unpleasant consequences (preoccupation with the drug to the exclusion of other interests and activities, being constantly under its influence or recovering from its effects, continuing to use it despite serious health risks and social penalties); and finally, two symptoms that imply a loss of freedom or psychological integrity (a persistent but ineffectual desire or repeated unsuccessful efforts to cut down one's use of the drug; and using the drug in larger amounts and for a longer time than intended). A diagnosis of addiction, for psychiatric purposes, requires the presence of any three of these seven symptoms.[107]

It is difficult to rank individual drugs by addictiveness, because so many other influences besides the pharmacology of the substance go into determining whether a person (or many people) will become addicted to a given drug, and because much depends on which aspect of addiction –

physiological responses, social consequences, health consequences, or compulsive use – is emphasised. Any attempt to rank drugs in this respect is bound to be subjective and controversial. With these reservations, the following table provides a rough ordering of addictive risk for some of the drugs most commonly used for non-medical purposes.

Table 1   Comparative dangers of various drugs

	Risk of compulsive use	Physical health risks	Behavioural and social risks	Tolerance and withdrawal reactions
Nicotine (Tobacco)	Very high	Very high	Very high	Moderate
Cocaine	Very high	High to moderate	High	High to moderate
Heroin	Very high	High to moderate	High	Very high
Methamphetamine	Very high	High to moderate	High	High to moderate
Caffeine	High	Very low	Very low	High to moderate
Alcohol (ethanol)	High to moderate	Very high	Very high	Very high
Cannabis	Moderate to low	Low	Low	Low
Diazepam (Valium)	Low	Low	Low	High to moderate
MDMA (Ecstasy)	Low	Uncertain	Moderate to low	Low
LSD	Very low	Low	Moderate	Very low

Evidence from neuroscience

If there is anything new in this field, it is what neuroscientists are learning about the way addiction works in the brain. Unlike most conditions defined as psychiatric disorders, drug addiction (or something like it) can be reliably produced and easily recognized in animals. Healthy laboratory rats will voluntarily take only a few non-nutritious chemicals, the same substances to which human beings become addicted; even their patterns of use resemble human addictive patterns, drug by drug. The target of these chemicals is a circuit that runs between the midbrain and the prefrontal region of the cerebral cortex. The central link in this circuit, which joins regions known as the ventral tegmental area (VTA) and nucleus accumbens (NAC), is the medial forebrain bundle. The NAC is part of the basal forebrain, which also contains the seat of planning and judgement in the prefrontal cortex, as well as the amygdala, sometimes described as a factory of the emotions. Both the NAC and the VTA are also regarded as part of the corpus striatum, which is involved in the programming of both body movements and thoughts.

This circuit is a reward system. It sets priorities for the organism by promoting actions needed for survival and reproduction. It regulates motivation, allowing us to learn, at a level below the reasonings of the cerebral cortex, what to seek and what to avoid. Stimulation of the NAC or its equivalent serves as a strong positive reinforcer in human beings and other creatures – even, apparently, insects and clams. It not only gives pleasure but, more important, strongly suggests: 'do that again'. Through the prefrontal cortex we learn about the world and develop expectations based on experience. Through its link to the NAC, these expectations are compared with stimuli the brain is receiving at any given moment. If the reward is greater than expected, the basal forebrain signals for action to continue receiving stimulus. In this way we lay down unconscious memories, reconcile desires with expectations, and develop motives for action.

Addictive drugs can capture this system and subvert it. Rats will press a lever repeatedly for intravenous injections of cocaine or heroin, just as they do for direct stimulation of the NAC by an implanted electrode. They have 'drunk the milk of Paradise', as the addict Coleridge wrote in his great poem about an opium dream. If the drug is supplied in unlimited amounts for a sufficient time and then taken away, the rat will press frantically for a while before giving up. For some time after that, it may not work even for direct stimulation of the brain. It has become temporarily insensitive to normal rewards.[108]

When addictive drugs disturb natural feedback and control in the reward circuit, they may cause long-lasting changes in its functioning. As the brain adapts to the onslaught of the drug, tolerance rises, and eventually, often, pleasure is almost absent or outweighed by misery. But the addict still wants the drug, because most other experiences have become even less rewarding. Liking and wanting have become separated.[109]

Addiction is not the same as physical dependence, exemplified in heroin and alcohol withdrawal reactions. Stimulant drugs, which are equally addictive, do not cause equally severe physical withdrawal reactions. The vast majority of patients who take high doses of an opiate for severe pain, even if they eventually suffer a typical withdrawal reaction, have no desire or tendency to go on taking the drug. As a well-known study by Lee Robins and her colleagues revealed, the same was true of most soldiers who used heroin in Vietnam.[110] Physical dependence in this sense is not linked to the reward and motivation system.[111]

A better indicator of addiction than physical dependence is 'craving'. The symptoms of craving may include irritable restlessness, indeterminate physical discomfort, mild depression, and a feeling that the drug will somehow provide relief. This state has proved very difficult to describe convincingly or measure accurately, but the underlying vulnerability is persistent. A single dose of the drug itself may be enough to re-establish the craving, even after years of abstinence. This is the so-called abstinence violation effect, which Alcoholics Anonymous acknowledges in the motto, 'It's the first drink that gets you drunk.'

One reason for the persistence of the addictive urge is conditioning or associative learning. In this process, previously neutral stimuli become cues that evoke a desire for the drug. The contexts in which the drug has been taken are never completely forgotten by the subcortical brain. Members of AA are told to avoid 'people, places, and things' associated with alcohol, because almost any of these may become a conditioned stimulus. Place preference is a type of conditioning often used in animal experiments. An animal will often take the drug more readily when it is returned to the environment where it became addicted – like an alcoholic who passes a familiar bar or a heroin addict who sees the street corner where he used to wait for a connection. It is as though the brain preserves an implicit memory of its predilection that is always available for retrieval.[112]

Addiction does not even require a drug, because any activity can affect the reward system and associative learning is a universal phenomenon. Injecting a drug may be the quickest, most direct, and often most unhealthy and socially destructive way to disturb motivation, and certainly it is the easiest way to study the system in animals. The unusual power, persistence, and devastating effects of certain drug habits have always been understood; for hundreds of years the general term 'intemperance' has been used for what we now usually call alcoholism. But pathological gambling and other consuming habits are sometimes called addictions, and many other devotions and commitments are unreasonable and self-destructive. Words like 'compulsion' and 'craving' can be applied to eating, sex, or love of another person. Drug withdrawal reactions and tolerance also have parallels in other forms of compensatory response and adaptation.

Thus although neuroscience has revealed interesting facts about the way addiction works in the brain, it cannot on its own explain what addiction is. Addiction has physiological concomitants, but it is not a purely physiological condition. The vast majority of drug users – even cocaine and heroin users – never become addicted. Many other circumstances determine whether or not a person will use a drug in a compulsive way. Individual differences in susceptibility arise from heredity, culture, and social conditions. Robins showed that most men who used heroin in Vietnam, even if they took it as much and as often as stateside addicts, had no tendency to relapse into addiction after returning to the United States. The men who did relapse usually had drug or alcohol problems and criminal records before joining the Armed Forces. Even rats have individual characteristics that affect their vulnerability to addiction.

Individual and social susceptibility

Heredity is a strong influence on sensitivity to the addictive powers of drugs. Different strains of rats and mice prefer different drugs. At a given dose of alcohol, the sons of alcoholic parents feel less intoxicated than average, and their posture and gait are altered less. This apparent resistance, also found in susceptible rats, is an early sign of vulnerability to alcoholism. Some people genetically at risk for addiction may have a congenitally high level of stress hormones or an abnormality in neurotransmitter activity – possibly some deficiency in the dopamine reward system – that is temporarily corrected by their drug of choice.

There are many genetic routes to addiction. For example, alcohol addicts are often divided into two classes. Type I alcoholics are usually male, vulnerable to drug addiction of all kinds, and inclined to antisocial behaviour. Type II alcoholics, whose symptoms are usually less severe and arise at a later age, are more often female and rarely have antisocial tendencies. Studies of adopted children and their biological families suggest that these types are genetically distinct.[113]

Social circumstances influence vulnerability and resistance to addiction in many ways. Isolated rats take more of an addictive drug than animals living in normal rat colonies. If human beings differ more than laboratory rats in individual susceptibility, it is not only because their brains are more complex but also because they live in more varied environments. People are most vulnerable to addiction if they lack significant capacities, interests and choices, other ways to solve problems and other sources of attachment. The brain's motivational system is more easily disturbed when its balance is not preserved by varied sources of reward and expectation. In this way, a person's addictive potential is affected by economic conditions, cultural traditions, formal and informal social controls, and the companionship and approval of other drug users.

And, of course, enough of the drug must be available to sustain an addiction. Among hunter-gatherers at the dawn of humanity, individual differences in susceptibility were probably unimportant, because it was almost impossible to get too much of a drug. The industrial age has brought with it mass production of drugs in their most concentrated and therefore most addictive forms, along with dangerous new synthetic drugs and a new method (intravenous injection) of gaining access to the brain. These are changes to which human beings have not had time to make a biological adaptation. There is a parallel with fatty foods, sugar and salt. These substances, necessary for life, were rare and difficult to find in the environment in which human beings evolved, so they supply a powerful stimulus to the reward system. Now that they are so freely available to many of us, excessive consumption and 'addictive' health risks are difficult to avoid.[114]

Perplexities of treatment

The variety of methods used to treat or control addiction reveals the ambiguities and uncertainties in our understanding of this condition. Despite our improved knowledge of the brain circuitry involved, chemical or biological treatments are not yet available and may never be. There are fairly effective drug treatments for some secondary symptoms, especially acute physical withdrawal reactions. We also have drugs that neutralise the pleasurable effects of opiates and alcohol. Disulfiram (Antabuse) prevents the digestive system from assimilating alcohol, making drinkers nauseated and sometimes seriously ill. Naltrexone and naloxone block receptors for the action of opiates and alcohol. Now researchers are trying to develop drugs that modify dopamine activity to prevent addiction while preserving normal function. They are also considering drugs that raise the level of inhibitory neurotransmitters, possibly reducing conditioned responses to drug-related cues. A vaccine for cocaine has been developed and is being tested.[115] But the only more or less proven chemical treatments now available involve the substitution of less harmful addictions: oral methadone for intravenous heroin, nicotine patches for cigarettes. Most established and prevalent treatments are non-chemical: residential therapeutic communities, inpatient chemical dependency treatment for alcoholism, and various forms of psychotherapy, behaviour therapy, counselling and social service.

Most addiction treatment programmes cooperate with self-help groups, the most important of which is Alcoholics Anonymous (now accommodating illicit drug users as well as alcoholics). The 12-step process that made AA famous involves admitting powerlessness, seeking help from a higher power, invoking it by meditation or prayer, taking a 'moral inventory', confessing wrongs, begging forgiveness, making amends, and carrying the message to others. The rules are: be honest about your problem, take responsibility, change yourself and help others – for your sake as well as theirs. According to Alcoholics Anonymous, anyone who has once been an alcoholic is always an alcoholic – 'always recovering, never recovered.'

Other programmes take a different approach, one that is based on behavioural and cognitive theories derived largely from the treatment of phobias and compulsive rituals. Drug abuse is regarded as behaviour encouraged by certain habits of thinking (cognitive therapy) or learned through patterns of conditioned association and reinforcement (behaviour therapy). Patients are exposed to situations, thoughts, and feelings that cause addictive use of drugs and efforts are made to prevent the usual responses. They work on stimuli and associations (classical conditioning) and incentives and consequences (operant conditioning). The purpose is to modify the abusive habit, either by making the drug less attractive or by creating rewarding alternatives.

Cognitive-behavioural approaches and Alcoholics Anonymous embody different ideas about the nature of drug addiction. AA demands self-surrender and self-renewal; the language of cognitive and behavioural therapy is less dramatic. AA seems to have more or less the same solution for everyone; in cognitive and behavioural treatment the goal is different for each person. Behavioural and cognitive therapists are less committed to total abstinence and not so insistent that patients define themselves as addicts. But there are many similarities as well: the demand for a drastic change in behaviour, the need to correct thinking (AA insists that its members avoid rationalisation and denial by declaring 'I am an alcoholic'); the notion of an abstinence violation effect ('It's the first drink that gets you drunk'); the need to take a personal inventory and consider long-term consequences ('Think through the drink', AA recommends); and the need to avoid cues for drinking or drug use ('people, places, and things' associated with alcohol, in AA's version). Members of AA supply one another with what behaviour therapists, using their own awkward language, might call modelling and corrective reinforcement, leading to self-efficacy.

The most serious obstacle to effective drug treatment is the unwillingness of addicts to take it seriously, even when they say they want it. They deny, conceal, rationalise, minimise and blame others. Even those who demand some kind of help may hope it will not require their giving up the drug habit. For example, heroin addicts usually refuse to take naltrexone for long, and alcoholics often discard Antabuse. By taking these drugs they can arrange to prevent themselves from feeling pleasure when they use alcohol or heroin. What they cannot do is prevent themselves from desiring alcohol or heroin. The heart of addiction lies in this ambivalence.

As William James once pointed out, we can often renounce the immediate satisfaction of a desire for the sake of long-term health and happiness if we group the desire with others in a general category and make a rule that applies to them all. Addiction often persists because the addict is unwilling or unable (here the distinction becomes doubtful) to acknowledge the kind of problem it is, the category to which it belongs. That is what is meant by denial. For each of the many situations and moods in which they are impelled to take the drink or drug, addicts can supply a different justification or excuse. Often they can change only when they come to understand that all their many seemingly different reasons for drinking or taking drugs belong under the heading of addiction. That is one reason why Alcoholics Anonymous insists that its members repeatedly tell themselves and others, 'I am an alcoholic.'

But generalising in order to act on principle depends on coordination between the seat of planning and judgment in the prefrontal cortex and the centres of desire and reward in the medial forebrain bundle. Addiction itself impairs this coordination. When the addict and calls on reserves (presumably from intact pathways in the brain), acknowledges the problem, and seeks treatment, it may be not just a means to recovery but a sign that recovery has already begun, because judgement is reassuming control over motivation. This change can be described as 'conceptual reframing' (the language preferred by cognitive therapists) or, more dramatically, as a 'personal crisis and conversion'

(Alcoholics Anonymous). Persuading addicts to resolve their ambivalence and acknowledge the problem is the explicit purpose of motivational enhancement therapy, a treatment introduced in the last ten years.[116]

Evaluating treatments

There is surprisingly little evidence on how well any of the standard treatments works. Critics question the treatment research because it has so many limitations, including insufficient time for follow-up (six months is common, although several years or more may be necessary to confirm recovery) and a high dropout rate. Other problems are the many patients lost to follow-up, lack of independent evaluation, reliance on questionable information provided by drug users themselves, and inconsistent or uncertain standards for measuring the outcome. There are hardly any controlled studies in which patients are randomly assigned either to treatment or no treatment. This is an especially difficult problem, because the centrality of motivation in addiction implies that being interested in treatment is in itself a major sign of improvement. There is no doubt that addicts who complete any form of treatment are more likely to recover. But it is not clear whether they have changed as a result of completing the treatment, or completed the treatment because they were already prepared to change.

It has not been shown clearly that any one treatment is better than another. (The only exception is methadone maintenance, a substitute addiction.) Because different kinds of treatment all produce similarly modest results, there is some suspicion that they are all merely placebos. Critics cite studies suggesting that, at least in milder forms of drug addiction, elaborate therapies are no more effective than being told to read a brief self-help manual or listen to a half-hour talk.

Even if no treatment can be proved consistently superior for all forms of addiction, may some be better than others for certain kinds of problem? The National Institute on Alcoholism and Alcohol Abuse in the United States sponsored a nationwide study called Project Match in an attempt to answer this question. The experiment, which lasted eight years and recruited more than 1600 patients, was one of the largest clinical studies ever conducted. A third of the participants was given cognitive behavioural therapy, one session a week for three months. Another third was enrolled in a programme that prepared them for Alcoholics Anonymous, also in one session a week for three months. The last third received motivational enhancement therapy in four sessions during the same period. After one year the rate of improvement was the same in all three groups. Nor was one treatment better than another for any particular group of alcoholics, whether defined by age, race, sex, social class, the severity of the symptoms, or the duration of the problem.[117]

A further difficulty in evaluating treatments is presented by the fact that most addicts - even heroin addicts – eventually recover whether they are treated or not. When a group of self-treated alcoholics was interviewed, most said they stopped because they simply decided that alcohol was bad for them. About a third said that health problems, frightening experiences, accidents or blackouts persuaded them to quit. A few had moments of crisis and renewal arising from a spiritual experience or a disastrous event that served as a warning – losing a job, a husband or wife, being arrested or injured while driving drunk or developing a physical illness. More often it was a gradual accumulation of inconveniences and miseries: 'Things were building up'; 'I was sick and tired of it'; 'I didn't want to live that way anymore'. To prevent themselves from relapsing, they avoided persons, places, and situations that put them under pressure to drink, rehearsed what to do or say when asked to take a drink, and repeatedly reminded themselves why they had quit. They used lapses and relapses to inform themselves about how to maintain their success.[118] The resemblance between these informal procedures and the methods used by cognitive-behavioural therapists and Alcoholics Anonymous is obvious.

The indistinct boundaries of addiction

A major complication in the understanding of addictions is created by a situation so common that there is a psychiatric term devoted to it: dual diagnosis. What this implies is that most people addicted to alcohol or illicit drugs have other psychiatric disorders as well. The most common are depression, anxiety disorders, and personality disorders – especially borderline personality (impulsive, emotionally unstable, chronically angry, suicidal) and antisocial personality (callous, reckless, deceitful). Sometimes the psychiatric symptoms and the addiction have a common cause in heredity, family environment, or traumatic stress. Drug addiction can cause psychiatric symptoms, and psychiatric illness can impair judgement, promoting addiction. Some addictive drug use is a misguided attempt to treat anxiety or depression. Eventually the addiction and the psychiatric symptoms reinforce each other in a way that makes cause and effect difficult to distinguish. The addiction can mimic the symptoms of the psychiatric disorder or disguise its presence, and people with serious psychiatric disorders are often evasive about their drug problems. So making the dual diagnosis is often difficult, and treatment is even more difficult.

In fact, alcoholics and other drug addicts often need help of so many kinds that it is unclear whether drugs are the main problem. Patterns of abuse and dependence are complicated and individually variable. Much research suggests that the amount of drugs or alcohol people use is not closely correlated with the severity of their psychological and social problems. In the previously mentioned Robins study, it was found that two or three years after their return, despite the extremely high rate of addiction in Vietnam, veterans were no more likely to be dependent on heroin than comparable civilians. Even men who used heroin again after returning to the United States rarely became re-addicted. Robins concluded that many people who are described as heroin addicts in order to fit the mould of a drug treatment programme have so many other problems, most of them antedating the addiction, that 'treatment of addiction' is a hopelessly inadequate description of their needs.[119]

This theme is illustrated in what may be the greatest drama ever written by an American – Eugene O'Neill's autobiographical *Long Day's Journey into Night*. The mother of the depicted family is a morphine addict; her husband and adult sons heavy drinkers – probably, by the American Psychiatric Association's definition, alcohol abusers. At first her addiction is presented as a disease, like the tuberculosis of her younger son; the sons accuse their stingy father of causing it by hiring a cheap but incompetent doctor to attend her at childbirth. She says, 'One day long ago I found I could no longer call my soul my own.' But she also calls herself 'a lying dope fiend', and her younger son Edmund says that she takes the drug because of an unhappy marriage, 'to get beyond our reach.' (As a matter of fact, most people given morphine by doctors do not become addicts.) The men's alcoholism is more consistently presented as a problem of character and situation rather than something traceable to the powers of a chemical. The press of circumstance and the unfolding of character seem indistinguishable; no line can be easily drawn between what these people do and what is done to them. The revelations in the drama centre around drugs and the family at once. As the action ends, late at night, with Mary Tyrone in a narcotic trance and her husband and older son in a whiskey stupor, it seems that these addictions are not so much distinct illnesses as a way of life.

Conclusion

Some researchers have suggested that we may discover the molecular switch in the brain that converts the merely reckless voluntary drug user into a diseased and unfree addict. Were this true, we would have the best possible justification for forcing addicts to undergo treatment. To prevent the addict from fulfilling his immediate desires would be to free him. This is precisely the policy John Stuart Mill advocated for those who could not be guided by persuasion, in which class he included children and 'savages'. Perhaps drug addicts are 'savages' who must be forced to be free. But one purpose of this essay has been to suggest that there is no such molecular switch in the brain, the discovery of which would settle this question. Addiction is not definable in strictly physiological terms, and addicts cannot be put in the same class as children or 'savages'. Compulsory treatment for drug addiction is unjustified.

The fact that some drug use is both habitual and self-destructive does not necessarily remove it from the sphere of morality. All virtues and vices are habits; habits constitute our personalities. We cannot regard every self-destructive or seemingly immoral or unwanted habit as a form of enslavement. As the complexity of its description and the variety of its treatments proves, the habitual behaviour of drug addicts is not mechanical and uniform. Besides, acting on a powerful, unwanted, irrational, or immoral desire is succumbing to temptation, and our mythical paradigm of succumbing to temptation – Adam and Eve in the Garden of Eden – is also a paradigm of the exercise of free will. If addiction is a disease, it is the only one for which the best-known treatment is a series of meetings in which sufferers confess their misdeeds, exhort one another to change their ways, and vow to rebel against a malevolent force while allying themselves with a higher and virtuous power.

Given the complexity of addiction, its indistinct boundaries, and its sometimes indirect relationship to the pharmacological qualities of the addictive substance, any classificatory system that evaluates addictiveness drug by drug is bound to be crude and inadequate. Furthermore, policymakers must consider other dangers in drug use besides addiction, including accidents, violence, and other psychological or physical harm resulting from a single use of the drug. But it seems fair to say (see Table 1 above) that if addictiveness were the only issue, alcohol, nicotine (or, more precisely, smoked tobacco), heroin, and cocaine would have to be regarded as the most dangerous drugs. Cannabis and MDMA would be of much less concern, and the hallucinogens LSD and mescaline would be of no concern at all. It will not escape the reader's notice that, for historical and sociological reasons, these distinctions do not correspond to the current legal classifications.

PART III
Drugs in Society

5. DRUGS AND POVERTY

GEOFFREY PEARSON

The relationship between drugs and deprivation is one of the defining aspects of the 'drugs problem'. It is a relationship that was first recognised in the powerful tradition of North American social research as early as the fifties and sixties. Since the onset of the heroin epidemic that swept through many parts of Britain in the eighties – the legacy of which remains Britain's most serious drug problem – these relationships have been cemented in the UK. They also exist in many other parts of continental Europe. In the UK there was initially an extreme reluctance on the part of successive Conservative governments to accept any connection between drugs and deprivation. However, a central feature of New Labour's ten-year drugs strategy, announced in 1998, is its determination to tackle drugs, crime and social exclusion in tandem.

The aim of this essay is to review the evidence for these connections between drugs and poverty, to ask what might cause them to be inter-linked, and to examine the consequences of their troubled relationship. I will not argue that only poor people use illicit drugs. That is manifestly not the case; a staple feature of newspaper headlines is to depict the excessive appetites of the rich and famous, and to portray their downfall if they should succumb to addiction. And the so-called recreational use of soft drugs such as cannabis is now so commonplace as to be found within all sections of society, particularly, although not solely, among the young. However, where drugs such as heroin and crack-cocaine are concerned, the most serious concentrations of human difficulty are invariably found huddled together with unemployment, poverty, housing decay and other social disadvantages. It is these multiple social problems that are my concern.

The North American experience: from heroin to crack cocaine
In the immediate post-war years – long before Britain would encounter such problems – there were outbreaks of heroin misuse in cities such as Chicago and New York. These struck hardest in the poorest areas. For example, Chein et al., in their 1964 study of New York, *The Road to H,* found a concentration of juvenile delinquency and narcotics use in the most socio-economically deprived areas.[120] A retrospective study of earlier heroin outbreaks in Chicago also found a similar pattern.[121]

If pockets of heroin addiction were already established in some US cities in the late forties and fifties, it was in the late sixties that heroin misuse began to assume truly epidemic proportions. The relationship between serious drug-related problems and unemployment and poverty was even more emphatically reinforced. For example, Patrick Hughes and his research team in Chicago, combining epidemiological fact-finding and ethnographic field observation, mapped the multiple local heroin outbreaks that occurred in the city between 1967 and 1971. Their research indicated that 'the largest outbreaks occurred in economically disadvantaged communities', including Chicago's black 'South Side'.[122] Hughes also advanced the intriguing 'contagious disease' model of heroin epidemics, which usefully describes the way drug consumption can move rapidly within vulnerable neighbourhoods by means of friendship networks.[123]

In the mid-eighties, the crack-cocaine epidemic established itself in many North American cities. Once again this was found to be rooted most firmly in the poorest neighbourhoods – invariably amongst African-American or Hispanic Latino populations. A large amount of detailed empirical research has been done on the social constitution of American crack users.[124] These studies offer a vivid and devastating commentary on urban living in late twentieth century America. Not only are the links between serious drug misuse and social exclusion uniformly and deeply entrenched; they also intersect with a variety of other social difficulties: widespread homelessness, drug-related crime and violence – including high levels of lethal violence – and brutal domestic relations. The life-threatening AIDS epidemic ran along the conduits of intravenous drug injecting, crack misuse and the sex industry. The official policy response – in terms of the provision of health care, drugs prevention, needle-exchange schemes etc. – was slow and often reluctant, sometimes even non-existent. According to some commentators, the 'war on drugs' in America became a war on poor people, with unbelievably high rates of imprisonment among young black and Latino males.[125] American drug policy, viewed in this light, seems an uninviting cul-de-sac.

The British heroin epidemic of the 1980s and its long shadow

Britain was something of a 'late-developer' when it came to drug-related problems on this scale. A tolerant attitude had been adopted by the 1920s Rollestone Committee, which allowed medical practitioners to prescribe pharmaceutically pure heroin to registered addicts, who were in any case very few in number. A sharp upturn in heroin misuse in the sixties startled the authorities. The previous system was more tightly regulated and then abandoned. In retrospect, however, this was nothing more than a mini-epidemic, involving no more than a thousand or so addicts, and hardly reaching beyond 'swinging' London.

Britain's slumbering, almost non-existent encounter with drugs took a sudden and decisive alteration in the early eighties, when heroin became available in cheap and plentiful supply in many of our towns and cities. This heroin originated from the region of Afghanistan, Pakistan and Iran, and was associated with the novel practice of 'chasing the dragon' or inhaling the fumes of heroin heated on metal foil. The habit spread like wildfire in towns and cities in the north of England and Scotland, where heroin use had previously been unknown, as well as in areas of working class London. And it quickly became apparent that the new British heroin users, like their American counterparts, were most likely to be young people living in the poorest neighbourhoods and suffering high levels of unemployment and social deprivation.

One of the earliest indications of this was in Glasgow, where a social survey by Haw found that 'the majority of identified opiate users come from the poorest areas of the city'.[126] At roughly the same time, exploratory research in the north of England commissioned by the Health Education Council confirmed the tendency for heroin use to be concentrated among young unemployed people living on impoverished council estates. This was amply confirmed by the major research programme of the period, which focused on the heroin epidemic on the Wirral peninsula in Merseyside.[127]

The emergence of Britain's heroin problem coincided with the deep economic recession of the eighties, the de-industrialisation of the economy and high levels of youth unemployment. The British experience reproduced that of the US, with the most serious concentrations of heroin misuse living cheek-by-jowl with urban poverty. Although the heroin epidemic was initially associated with 'chasing the dragon', many users turned to self-injection as a more efficient means of using an expensive commodity. By the late eighties, the link with AIDS had come to be recognised as a vital public health issue. The British response was more forward looking than that of the US, however, and harm-reduction measures such as needle-exchange schemes proliferated throughout the UK. Finally, the drugs-crime link which had been such a dominant feature of the North American scene was cemented in Britain with estimates – albeit somewhat shaky on firm evidence – suggesting that as much as one-third of property crime in Britain is drug-related. However, there are important local and regional variations in patterns of availability and use of different drugs, which make it extremely difficult to generalise on the extent of the drugs-crime connection.[128]

As the earlier American experience had shown, heroin epidemics cast a long shadow. The legacy of the eighties heroin epidemic remains Britain's most significant drug problem. In addition, pockets of serious crack-cocaine misuse have made limited inroads in some communities, although we have less detailed evidence on crack-cocaine in the UK. In the course of the nineties, the geographical reach of heroin misuse widened. Small cities such as Bradford, Bristol and Hull, with no heroin history, began to report problems with the drug.[129] The ethnic contours of the problem have also begun to change. The profile of heroin users had initially been almost exclusively white working class – something that often astonishes American observers. More recently, there are signs that this monochrome pattern has begun to break up, with particularly worrying signs of increasing heroin use in Pakistani and Bangladeshi communities, where unsustainably high levels of youth unemployment are also to be found.[130] The inter-related difficulties of serious drug misuse, crime, disease and poverty have now become an indelible feature of the landscape.

Drugs and social deprivation: cause and effect

To better understand the coexistence of hard drug use and social deprivation, we must enquire into its causes. The first thing to note is that the connection is not limited to illegal drugs. Poor people not only take proportionately more heroin and crack cocaine; they also drink harder and smoke more. One explanation of this phenomenon is that those with meagre prospects tend to be less concerned about the long-term health risks posed by all these substances. Another hypothesis is that lack of external opportunity encourages the poor to seek the direct neurological excitation offered by drugs. It is interesting, in this connection, that laboratory animals are far more likely to become addicted to heroin and cocaine if they are deprived of other sources of stimulation.[131]

Other features of social deprivation give encouragement specifically to illegal drugs. One of these is housing policy. The large municipal estates erected in the fifties and sixties have led to the spatial concentration of social deprivation. Such estates gather the unemployed, the uneducated and single parents together in the same locality. They have become known as 'problem' or 'sink' estates. Similar difficulties exist in the urban ghettos of the USA, in the French *banlieues* and elsewhere.[132] Since, as Patrick Hughes and others have noted, illegal drugs tend to spread along friendship networks, the concentration of a large number of people vulnerable to drug addiction in the same neighbourhood encourages its rapid diffusion. This is one of the explanations for why drug abuse has always been a predominantly *metropolitan* problem.

Long-term unemployment also increases people's vulnerability to drug addiction. As Norman Zinberg has demonstrated, people with rewarding long-term projects – such as a job – are less likely to develop problems with drugs.[133] Such projects are incompatible with the more uncontrolled forms of drug taking; in their absence, exposure to drugs is likely to result in chaotic and compulsive patterns of use. It is no accident that the mid-eighties heroin epidemic coincided with unusually high levels of youth unemployment.

Associated with unemployment is the emergence of deviant and delinquent subcultures amongst young people. These have often been charted in North American and British criminology. They are subcultures of defiance and nihilism, but they also offer a means of demonstrating prowess, achievement and status for those who possess no such opportunities within the formal economy. And finally, of course, there are tangible gains to be made as low-level dealers in the drugs trade – economic incentives which do not begin to compare with those operating in the upper reaches of the drug market, but which can nevertheless prove attractive to the poor. Among such low-level dealers considerable entrepreneurial determination and flair is not uncommon.

While poverty and unemployment often lead to drug addiction, drug addiction can serve in turn to entrench poverty and unemployment. The common view of drug addiction as a form of idleness is wide of the mark; being a drug addict is a full-time career. The everyday routines necessary to sustain a heroin or cocaine habit are extremely demanding, requiring energy and commitment.[134] As well as a new way of life, addiction often brings with it a new circle of friends. The all-absorbing nature of addiction leaves little room for other relationships and projects, which are gradually abandoned. Someone who turns to heroin after losing a job or a partner will find it increasingly hard to find another job or another partner. The chain of reinforcement runs in both directions.

Powerful evidence for the interdependency of drug addiction and poverty is provided by the recent study of young heroin users by the drugs research centre SPARC. The study found that 'many of our subjects began their adolescence in tolerably supportive arrangements' but that 'their heroin careers ensured their social realignment was towards the margins'. The reasons for this downward drift are 'growing heroin dependency… and subsequent problems with personal health, expulsions, drugs bills, and an increasing reliance on acquisitive crime and drug dealing to supplement legitimate income.'[135]

It is not clear to what extent this effect is a consequence of the illegality of heroin and cocaine, rather than of the intrinsic properties of the drugs themselves. Addiction to heroin and cocaine is undoubtedly debilitating. But any damage wrought by addiction itself is magnified by policy. This is born out by the case of alcohol. Alcohol is not a harmless drug. But the disastrous US experiment with alcohol prohibition in the 1920s spawned a whole new set of problems – the creation of illicit drinking venues, the encouragement of violent criminal mafias, the corruption of police officers and the criminalisation of many otherwise law-abiding citizens who liked a tipple. All these problems are reoccurring today in connection with drug prohibition.

It is particularly noteworthy here that prohibition rebounds most heavily against the poor. Whereas wealthier addicts may be able to afford the high retail price of illicit drugs, poorer addicts are often forced into debt, crime or prostitution. The reasons for the social marginalisation of heroin users listed by the SPARC study quoted above – illness, expulsions, debt and crime – are all to a large extent consequences of heroin's illegality.

If prohibition helps to marginalise heroin addicts, this may in turn make it more difficult for them to give up the drug. Thus current policy may actually help to entrench the association between drug addiction and social deprivation. Important evidence for this hypothesis is provided by the 1994–1996 Swiss experiment in heroin prescription. Not only did the number of crimes committed by participants go down markedly; other indicators of social integration (such as permanent employment and housing) improved.[136]

A 'joined-up' drug strategy

In view of this complex web of causal relations, the goal of drug policy must be broadened. The aim must be not just to get users 'off drugs', but also to give them access to the benefits that will, hopefully, *keep* them off drugs. Drug policy must, in other words, take its place within a wider programme of urban regeneration. The present government's ten-year strategy is a step in this direction.

It is remarkable that the well-established connections between poverty, drug misuse and crime were ignored or denied for so long by British politicians. Lady Thatcher's pronouncement that 'there is no such thing as society' was reflected in the ways in which the social consequences of high unemployment were marginalised by successive Conservative administrations throughout the eighties and early nineties. It should be remembered that even the Archbishop of Canterbury's 1985 report *Faith in the City*, which examined the roots of disorder in Britain's impoverished inner cities, was decried by government ministers at the time as 'Marxism'.

The turning point came in the mid-nineties, when the government's relatively independent Advisory Council on the Misuse of Drugs established a working party to examine environmental influences on drug-related problems. This included a systematic review of the accumulated evidence on the relationship between drug misuse and social exclusion. The conclusions of its report, *Drug Misuse and the Environment*, were emphatic: 'We thus assert without any of the familiar hedging with 'on the one hand but on the other', that on strong balance of probability deprivation is today in Britain likely often to make a significant causal contribution to the cause, complication and intractability of damaging kinds of drug misuse... We want now and in the future to see deprivation given its full and proper place in all considerations of drug prevention policy, held in that policy consciousness, and not let slip from sight.'[137]

The Advisory Council's recognition that drug-related problems are closely inter-twined with social deprivation was thus a landmark in British social policy. This recognition is now formally enshrined in New Labour's ten-year drug strategy, announced in 1998. The ten-year strategy expresses New Labour's philosophy of 'joined-up' government; it aims, in the words of Tony Blair, to make the fight against drugs 'part of a wider range of policies to renew our communities'. The overall objective is 'to shift the emphasis away from dealing with the consequences of the problem, to actively preventing it happening in the first place.'[138]

The ten-year strategy makes several crucial innovations. It recognises for the first time that not all drug use is equally harmful. It therefore makes its primary target the harm associated with drug use, rather than drug use itself. It pursues a strategy of what is known as 'harm-reduction' as opposed to 'use-reduction'. In accordance with these aims, the government proposes to shift the burden of funding from measures aimed at reducing supply to measures aimed at reducing demand. Although spending on all items of the drug budget is projected to increase, spending on demand-side measures is planned to increase at a much greater rate than spending on supply-side measures. By the year 2002-3, as the following Treasury estimates show, 'treatment' will outstrip 'reducing availability' as the single largest item in the national drugs budget.

Table 1   Projected interdepartmental expenditure on UK drug policy measures, in pounds sterling[139]

| Year | Strategy Area | | | | |
	Drug treatment	Protecting young people	Safeguarding communities	Reducing availability	Total
2000-01	234	63	45	353	695
2001-02	328	90	79	373	870
2002-03	377	97	81	376	931
2003-04	401	120	95	380	996

Table 2   Projected interdepartmental expenditure on UK drug policy measures, as a percentage of the total

| Year | Strategy Area | | | | |
	Drug treatment	Protecting young people	Safeguarding communities	Reducing availability	Total
2000-01	34%	9%	6%	51%	100%
2001-02	38%	10%	9%	43%	100%
2002-03	40%	10%	9%	40%	100%
2003-04	40%	12%	10%	38%	100%

The principle that policy should be targeted at drug-related harm, rather than drug use *per se*, implies more protection for young people, for it is among them that drugs are believed to do most damage. Expenditure on 'protecting young people' is accordingly projected to double in the next four years. The target is to reduce the number of young people using heroin and cocaine by 25 per cent by 2005 and by 50 per cent by 2008. Most of the extra money will be spent on drug education programmes. Particularly significant, as an illustration of New Labour's determination to treat drugs as part of the wider problem of social exclusion, is the Positive Futures Initiative, which 'aims to divert vulnerable young people aged 10 to 16 years old into sport and healthy outdoor activities and away from drug misuse and anti-social activities.[140]

But the single largest increase in spending, in absolute terms, is on drug treatment. This emphasis is largely inspired by influential American studies arguing that treatment is the most efficient means of reducing the social costs of drug misuse, as measured against other interventions such as domestic enforcement or border interdiction.[141] Keith Hellawell confidently states: 'We know that treatment works. It is the only way to break the link between drugs and crime'.

One controversial aspect of New Labour's drugs strategy is its provision for what is known as 'coercive treatment'. Drug users who appear before the courts on charges of theft and burglary can be ordered to receive treatment for their drug problems and to submit to regular tests to ensure that they remain drug-free. Coercive treatment has been criticised as draconian, but it springs logically from an enlarged conception of harm-reduction. Much of the harm resulting from drug misuse is inflicted not only on the individual drug user and his or her immediate family, but also on non-drug using neighbours and the wider community. 'Harm-reduction' strategies must accordingly be broadened in scope. The early signs are that coercive treatment can help to reduce an individual's levels of drug consumption and hence his or her propensity to commit drug-related crime.[142] If the priority is to protect communities from drug-related crime and nuisance, then such treatment has some justification.

Conclusions

But although New Labour's drug policy is a great improvement over its predecessors, it could go further. As I have argued, the destructive social consequences of drug addiction are magnified by prohibition. If the government is serious about tackling these consequences, it had better re-examine the basic assumptions underlying prohibition. There is no need for access to dangerous substances to be controlled only by criminal sanctions. Other forms of control include prescription to registered addicts, licensing and taxation. All are worth considering.

I believe that the outright legalisation of all currently illicit drugs would be a rash experiment. Nonetheless, any rational drugs policy will admit that prohibition carries considerable costs, and will attempt to minimise those costs while at the same time retaining the benefits of control. One such attempt is found in Mark Kleiman's book, *Against Excess*, which provides a review of the likely costs and benefits resulting from different control regimes as applied to different drugs.[143] Vital to Kleiman's analysis, and to the argument advanced here, is that some drugs are much more harmful than others, and that different control regimes are therefore appropriate for different drugs.

The law against cannabis, above all others, cries out for reform. Cannabis is by far the most widely used illicit drug in Britain. Slightly more than fifty per cent of young people in Britain have now smoked cannabis at some point in their lives. Five million people aged between 16 and 29 have tried cannabis, and something like one-and-a-half to two million people in the same age group use the drug regularly.[144] In addition, there are largely unknown millions who smoke or have smoked cannabis in older age groups.[145] This widespread cannabis use is associated with relatively few social costs. Cannabis smoking is dispersed through society and does not have the close association with poverty and social exclusion observed for heroin and crack-cocaine. An editorial in *The Lancet* stated that 'on the medical evidence available, moderate indulgence in cannabis has little ill-effects on health'.[146]

Yet cannabis currently absorbs a large amount of the total police time devoted towards illicit drug control. Something like 80-85 per cent of all drug-related arrests are for possession of cannabis for personal use. This is an absurd state of affairs. The law as it is currently applied focuses on the least harmful of illicit drugs. It therefore works in direct opposition to the fundamental principle of the government's own drugs strategy, which is 'to focus on those [drugs] that cause the greatest damage'.[147]

Not only does the current law on cannabis waste resources that could be devoted to tackling truly dangerous drugs; it also directly impedes the effort to deal with those drugs. We know surprisingly little about the social characteristics of those arrested for cannabis offences. But we do know that the vast majority of drug possession offences arise from police stop-and-search, and that stop-and-search powers are used disproportionately against the young and those from ethnic minorities. It seems reasonable to assume that the current application of cannabis laws serves only to further alienate members of these groups from the law. Yet these are precisely the communities in which it is vitally important that the police and other social agencies are seen as allies in the struggle against heroin and crack-cocaine. Only then can the government achieve the real aim of drug policy, summed up by Bruce Jacobs as the 'reintegration into normal society' of 'those who may never have been integrated in the first place'.[148]

6. DRUGS IN JAIL

IAN MCLAUGHLIN

I am a forty-two year man who has used various illegal as well as prescription drugs from the age of thirteen onwards. I have spent a similar period of time in one or another institution, including twenty of the last twenty-five years in and out of various prisons.

Strange though it may seem, given the much-talked about link between drugs and crime, not a single one of my hundreds of offences, both inside and outside prison, was in any way drugs-related.

Over the course of my life I have seen massive changes in the number of drug users, the culture surrounding drugs, and in society's perception of drug users. Indeed, my own views on drugs and drug users have changed drastically, especially in the past six or seven years.

At the age of twelve or thirteen I started sniffing glue and other solvents, petrol from the school lawnmower and even chloroform from the biology lab. These initial excursions were very short lived, due to one of the boys in our group going into a coma after sniffing Evo-stick. Of the seven or eight who indulged this particular practice, all but two were scared off by this boy's unfortunate experience.

A year or so later I smoked cannabis (or at least it was supposed to be cannabis!) for the first time. The children's home I was in had a resident 'junkie' who encouraged three or four of us to share a couple of spliffs with him. We knew he was a junkie because he had long hair, wore hippy clothes, and every two or three weeks appeared with a couple of spliffs. He was only a year or so older than us, but a real rebel in our eyes. I must admit that these first few tastes of cannabis did absolutely nothing for me nor, I suspect, for the others, but we all sat around making a big show of acting 'stoned' and everything being 'far out man'. For a few months we all pooled our pocket money every few weeks in order to buy a few spliffs from this 'junkie'. We got 'wrecked', 'wasted' or 'smashed', listened to heavy metal and wished love and peace on the world. I distinctly remember being given a wide berth by others, who thought we were contaminated in some way, and generally treated us with contempt.

Again, this early foray into the world of drugs was short-lived. It was superseded by the discovery that there were certain pubs in the area where a few of us could be served under-age. It quickly became apparent that a couple of weeks pocket money enabled us to go out, get pissed out of our minds and stagger back home to a right old bollocking and grounding from the headmaster. Oh yes, in contrast to our spliff-smoking phase, we quickly became heroes to our peers. Cloths covered in vomit, bloody and torn from fighting, were badges to be worn with honour.

For several years I carried on drinking more heavily than was good for me, often stealing to fund a social life spent mainly in pubs and nightclubs. I rarely took drugs during this period, apart from the occasional spliff or 'backstreet blue' (speed tablet) at parties. The most noticeable exception was my first experience with LSD. This was incredibly hallucinatory, as you might expect of the acid of that period. It has never been the same since 'Operation Julie' smashed almost all the illegal LSD labs in Britain. What today's generation thinks of as acid is in fact mainly amphetamine based.

Throughout this period, and up until the late seventies, the drug culture seemed to be mainly confined to a small group of (young) people. Drug users looked very much like the stereotype of drug users, with hippy clothes, long hair etc. Drug related crime was almost non-existent.

I have spent most of these last twenty years in prison, but from this vantage point I have been able to observe the changes that have taken place in society as a whole. Prison is, after all, only a concentrated reflection of the world outside! Starting in the early eighties, there was been a significant rise in the number of youngsters jailed either for drug offences or for offences committed to fund their drug taking. From this time too the use of cannabis in prisons became more widespread, at first among younger prisoners, but then gradually among the prison population as a whole. Amphetamines and heroin were also on the increase, especially in the large city prisons.

It was when I first served in an adult prison that I came into contact with heroin addicts. In the main, they seemed to be a throwback to the sixties. They were easily identifiable by their 'hippy' uniform and lifestyle, as well as by the fact that most of them had to do their 'turkey' upon reception before being allowed to settle into their sentences. But this slowly changed. More and more people with different lifestyles started taking drugs. Now you can no longer tell by looking at someone whether they do drugs or not.

The most noticeable consequence of the spread of drugs was a dramatic change in the pecking order within prisons. Whereas before it was the tobacco barons who held sway, now any inmate who happened to have access to large amounts of drugs could exert influence over other inmates. But there as yet didn't appear to be any organised suppliers operating in prisons. There was still an aversion to drugs among the old-time villains.

However, it wasn't long before the so-called 'top-villains' or gangsters started to take control of the supply, both inside and outside prison. These old-time criminals, traditionally associated with armed-robbery and such like, once again rose to the top of the prison pecking order by selling drugs. With them occupying the top tiers, and a growing number of cannabis and heroin users at the bottom, various levels of 'collectors', 'runners', 'bankers' and 'enforcers' emerged to complete the pyramid.

At first the authorities seemed to be very frightened about the growing influx of cannabis into jails, meting out severe punishments for people caught in possession. But over time they became more relaxed. Although they still made occasional token efforts, by and large they were happy to maintain the status quo. It was accepted that drugs had a calming influence on prisoners, making them easier to control. When action was taken, it was invariably directed against those at the bottom of the pyramid. This was for two reasons. First, users at the bottom of the pyramid were easier to identify. Secondly, by acting against the barons at the top the authorities risked creating a power vacuum, which might then lead to gang violence.

One method used by the drug barons to retain control of the market was informing. Group X might inform on group Y, with the aim of taking over its business. Group X might even plant drugs on members of group Y, letting the authorities know how they might be found. It was almost laughable for us at the bottom of the pyramid to watch these gangsters getting away with the very same things for which we were persecuted. We were often acting out of desperation; they were acting out of greed.

In the nineties, heroin replaced cannabis as the most popular drug in prisons. This was largely an unintended consequence of the introduction of mandatory drug testing in the mid-nineties. Whereas cannabis shows up in these tests for up to twenty-eight days after use, heroin clears the body after three or four days. Heroin has become the favoured drug of suppliers as well; it is easier to smuggle into prisons than cannabis, being less bulky, and the profits are astronomical. In some of the higher security category jails it is possible to obtain limitless amounts of heroin, whereas cannabis is all but unobtainable.

Depending on their security classification, different prisons have slightly different price structures, with lower prices in lower category jails. In general though, cannabis sells for two to two-and-a-half times the street price, whereas heroin sells for around six times street price. And often the heroin is further adulterated in prison, increasing both the level of profit and the risk to health.

Let me illustrate the difference between the two drugs with a concrete example. A matchbox will hold about an ounce of cannabis, which costs £80 to £90 outside and would sell, at the bottom of the pyramid, for £200 to £250. By comparison, an ounce of heroin can be bought outside for £700 to £800 and can earn, again at the bottom of the pyramid, £5,500 to £6,000 – even more if it is adulterated. What supplier would not prefer heroin to cannabis?

How do prisoners find the money to pay for drugs? The average wage in prison is around £6.50 a week. In 'working prisons' this is a lot higher, sometimes around £20 a week. On top of that, I estimate that at least a third of inmates have access to £10-£15 from outside, known as 'private spends'. So in a jail of 500 inmates there is about £6,000 available to spend in an average week. From experience, I would say that about half of this is spent on drugs. No cash actually swaps hands. Prisoners receive money in the form of credit, to be exchanged for cigarettes, phone-cards and other 'luxury goods' from the canteen. These items play an important role in financing drug deals at the bottom of the pyramid. Obviously, those at the top of the pyramid have no need for such trivia, so they are swapped and sold for cash or jewellery.

In addition, it soon becomes obvious to the drug barons which inmates have access to money outside. These people are 'targeted' and given extended lines of credit – to be settled outside. I have seen prisoners at the bottom of the pyramid fighting in the visiting rooms with their wives or girlfriends, because they haven't given over a large part of their weekly benefits to pay for drugs. If these wives or girlfriends refuse to pay they are sometimes robbed of their possessions outside prison. Because dealers and addicts are often from the same estate, it is easy for the dealers to maintain their trade through intimidation and fear.

When an inmate has no one outside to finance his addiction he has two options. He can move up the pyramid, buying 'wholesale' and selling on, using the profit to feed his own habit. Otherwise he must run up debt, in which case he is eventually forced to segregate himself for his own protection. The most insidious consequence of all this is the culture of violence, bullying and intimidation that now prevails in most prisons.

Very recently I have spent time in two lower category prisons. In the first, heroin use was already high among the 450 inmates. There were several main 'barons', each with his own pyramid. These pyramids often overlapped at the lower levels, as the barons competed for business, creating all kinds of tension. Violence was an everyday occurrence, with gangs of heavies assaulting inmates who couldn't pay debts, stealing drugs from inmates who had obtained them from another supplier, and fighting other gangs who were trying to 'poach their customers'. There was hardly a prisoner who wasn't, to one degree or another, affected by the prevailing drug culture. If the authorities moved against a particular gang the levels of violence and intimidation merely increased! I spoke to a number of staff who were well aware of what was going on. They were convinced it was a volcano ready to erupt.

The second of the two prisons had a reputation for being very relaxed, with hardly any violence and good relations between staff and inmates. Inmates were allocated there as a reward for previous good behaviour, and after being assessed as suitable for the relaxed regime. It soon became obvious that the prison no longer warranted this good reputation. Heroin, and the whole culture associated with it, had gained a foothold there. By the time I left it seemed to be touch and go as to whether the authorities could stamp out drugs and reassert control. But previous experience leads me to believe that they will fail.

I haven't been outside since 1990, but I can well imagine that certain deprived estates are no different from prisons, with the whole cycle of addiction, crime, violence and intimidation effecting drug users and non-drug users alike. I read that the authorities now provide drug counsellors at police stations, probation offices and courts, and that people arrested are to be drug tested. Frankly, this is the same as sticking plaster on a crumbling dam. Do these smug mandarins really believe that a mere test, or an hour's counselling, can change the way of life of someone brought up knowing nothing except drugs and crime? Over the past few years the authorities have also provided counselling and courses within prison, but it has been no way near enough to combat the problem. There are some excellent drug rehabilitation units in prison, but they are only available to a tiny proportion of the inmates who urgently need them. The three-day drug courses that are being run don't have any effect whatsoever; a lot of prisoners only attend them in order to gain home-leave, parole etc.

For years I advocated legalising cannabis, while strengthening the law against hard drugs. During the past six years, however, I have experienced two periods of addiction to heroin, and this has changed my attitude. Although these episodes lasted only a couple of months each, after which time I managed to pull myself away, during those periods I went through living hell. The worst thing was falling into the clutches of the dealers. On the first occasion I tried to finance my addiction by moving up the pyramid, but very quickly found I couldn't bring myself to inflict on others the misery I was inflicting on myself. On the second occasion I allowed my debt to build up until it was out of control. Both times I had to segregate myself from the people who controlled the drug that I had allowed to control me.

I now firmly believe that *all* illegal drugs must be decriminalised, for the sake of the huge number of drug users and the victims they create. Drugs *must* be taken out of the hands of criminal suppliers. They should be made available on prescription, at affordable prices, to all users. This is with the proviso that users undergo education into the risks of drug use, and receive real long-term counselling to deal with the problems underlying their need to use drugs. I fear that politicians will not find the moral courage to take these drastic steps, but unless they reverse the failed policy of trying to eradicate drugs entirely, everyone will suffer the consequences.

PART IV
Alternatives for Policy

7. COMMON SENSE ON CANNABIS

PETER LILLEY

The decriminalisation of cannabis is inevitable. Indeed, it is happening already. In many parts of the country the police no longer prosecute cannabis users. The problem is not simply that the current law is unenforceable – it is also indefensible. The arguments for criminalisation of cannabis that we hear so often crumble on analysis. Laws that can neither be enforced nor defended cannot survive.

This is not to say that cannabis use is inconsequential. Like alcohol, cannabis can be abused. But the fact of abuse does not furnish a sufficient reason for prohibiting all consumption of either substance. If the present legal status of cannabis use is unsustainable and undesirable one must then confront the daunting question of how we move to a more sensible situation without appearing to confer public approval on cannabis use and abuse.

The current situation is characterised by the wilful confusion of the immoral and the illegal, of use and abuse and of soft and hard drugs. As a result, legalisation of cannabis use is often misrepresented as a softening of moral attitudes and policy on not simply the consumption of cannabis but hard drugs as well. That is why the issue is such a political hot potato, and why few prominent politicians have been willing to speak out publicly in favour of change. Nonetheless, it is clear that even those members of the public most likely to oppose drug-taking – the adult and conservative – recognise a difference between using cannabis and hard drugs.

The removal of legal penalties need not imply public approval of cannabis use, still less of abuse. It is for the individual to exercise personal responsibility in the use of cannabis as of alcohol. And it is for parents, teachers and pastors to teach what is right in this area, not for the law or politicians to curtail our freedom to act responsibly. Above all, we should recognise that penalisation of cannabis use, far from preventing people sliding down the slippery slope from soft drugs to hard drugs, actually makes that descent more likely. It brings the soft drug user into contact with the hard drug pusher, since both types of drug are forced through the same illegal channels. The most important objective of changing the law on cannabis must be to break this link.

Cannabis usage
Cannabis is by far the most widely used illegal drug, particularly among the

young. Some 17 per cent of young people aged between 16 and 24 claim to have taken cannabis within the last month and 43 per cent of this age group say they have tried cannabis at some stage in their life. Some 1.25 million people in the UK claim to have taken cannabis in the last month.

This level of usage is substantially greater than the level of usage of all other controlled drugs combined. It totally dwarfs usage of hard drugs. For every person using heroin there may be some one hundred people who use cannabis. However, cannabis usage is still well below that of legal 'drugs' like alcohol and tobacco. Over a quarter of people aged 16 and above smoke cigarettes and over half drink alcohol once or more a week.

The current law

Over 40 per cent of young people have defied the law by taking cannabis despite the existence of fairly severe penalties. The *Misuse of Drugs Act 1971* creates three classes of controlled drugs:

- Class A comprises the hard drugs like heroin and cocaine as well as hallucinogens like LSD and Ecstasy.
- Class B comprises cannabis along with amphetamines and barbiturates.
- Class C includes tranquillisers and mild opioid analgesics.

Offences involving class A drugs involve the highest penalties ranging up to life sentences and/or unlimited fines for trafficking. Offences involving class B drugs also carry severe penalties. Cultivation, production, supplying, being responsible for a property used for any of these activities and possession with intent to supply carry maximum penalties of 14 years or a fine or both if tried in a Crown Court. In a Magistrates Court the maximum sentences for these offences are six months or a £5,000 fine or both. Possession for own use can carry a potential punishment of up to five years and/or a fine if tried in a Crown Court. More typically such offences are dealt with by a Magistrates Court in which the maximum sentence would be three months or a £2,500 fine or both.

These penalties have not prevented widespread use of cannabis with the result that increasing numbers of people have fallen foul of the drugs laws. The number of people arrested for offences involving cannabis nearly quadrupled from 26,000 to 97,000 in the ten-year period from 1988 to 1998.

However, the police and the courts are enforcing the laws against cannabis with diminishing enthusiasm. As the number of arrests has grown the proportion of people let off with a caution has risen from under a third in 1988 to over half in recent years. And the proportion of those who are found guilty by the courts has declined from nearly two-thirds to under half. A survey carried out for a Panorama programme broadcast in November 1999 found that two-thirds of police officers would no longer prosecute someone for having a few cannabis plants. Indeed, most police officers surveyed believed cannabis to be far less harmful or addictive than alcohol or tobacco. The decision by the Police Commander for Lambeth in July 2001 not to pursue minor cannabis offences so as to release officers to tackle more important crimes shows how *de facto* depenalisation is gathering pace.

History of UK policy on cannabis
In the nineteenth century cannabis was not an issue within the UK. The first British interest in cannabis use was in India over a century ago. Concern had been expressed in Parliament about native use of Indian hemp – the local form of cannabis. So the Indian authorities set up the Indian Hemp Drugs Commission that reported in 1894. Although the first study ever carried out it was one of the most thorough. It concluded 'that the excessive use (of hemp) is comparatively exceptional' and that 'moderate use produces practically no ill effects.' The Indian government accepted the report's recommendations that Indian hemp use should be controlled by taxes rather than prohibited.

Laws controlling hard drugs were only introduced in Britain following a series of international conferences early in the 20th century. The Hague Convention of 1912 bound its 34 signatories to tighten control on opiates and cocaine but did not include cannabis.. So the first (peacetime) British drug law – the Dangerous Drugs Act 1920 – which belatedly implemented the convention did not cover cannabis.

However, at the second conference held in Geneva in 1924 the Egyptian government insisted that cannabis be added to the list of drugs subject to international control. This was duly done and for the first time cannabis became a controlled drug in the UK under the Dangerous Drugs Act 1925. A third international convention – the 1961 Single Convention On Narcotic Drugs hosted by the United Nations – consolidated and strengthened international agreements on drugs control and was ratified by the UK in 1964. It is still the 1961 convention that requires Britain to control trade in cannabis, along with cocaine and heroin. Control does not necessarily mean criminalisation of cultivation, sale and possession – it can mean some form of regulation of these activities. However, the Dangerous Drugs Act 1964 which gave effect to the convention's provisions duly made it an offence to cultivate cannabis or to permit premises to be used for smoking or dealing in cannabis.

Arguments for criminalising cannabis

Although cannabis was swept into the scope of our drugs laws in the slipstream of hard drugs like opium, heroin and cocaine with little serious thought, its retention is now justified by a number of claims about the consequences of cannabis use. These are that

(i)   Cannabis is seriously addictive

(ii) Cannabis is hazardous to health

(iii) Cannabis generates damaging behavioural consequences

(iv) Cannabis leads to use of hard drugs

(v) Cannabis use is immoral.

But even if these claims are true, it does not necessarily follow that cannabis use should be criminalised. Almost no substance that human beings consume is entirely devoid of adverse consequences. So the crucial question with regard to cannabis is: are the negative effects of its use sufficiently severe and widespread to justify prohibition, particularly in a country that permits the sale of alcohol and tobacco? Let us examine the claims in turn.

(i) 'Cannabis is seriously addictive'

Serious cannabis dependency is sufficiently rare that its existence has been disputed. In any case, it appears to be a problem only among heavy and persistent users. Cannabis does not have the physical addictive power of heroin nor the propensity to induce dependence on the same scale as nicotine or alcohol.

A recent comprehensive review of scientific research on cannabis published in the Lancet in 1998 concluded that 'some heavy smokers of cannabis report withdrawal symptoms on the abrupt cessation of cannabis use. There is evidence that a cannabis dependency syndrome occurs with heavy chronic use.... About one in 10 of those who ever use cannabis become dependent on it at some time during their four or five years of heaviest use. This risk is more like the equivalent risk for alcohol (15 per cent) than for nicotine (32 per cent) or opioids (23 per cent).'[149]

The numbers of cannabis users reporting to drug dependency clinics is sometimes used to suggest that cannabis is a major problem. In fact, those citing cannabis as their main drug constitute about 10 per cent of all referrals, even though cannabis is overwhelmingly the most frequently used drug. Moreover, some of those citing cannabis may be reluctant initially to admit to dependence on other drugs that they are also taking.

(ii) 'Cannabis is hazardous to health'

The alleged health risks of cannabis use are often cited by the Labour government in defence of the current laws. It is worth quoting at length the Home Office minister, Charles Clarke, in the parliamentary debate on the 12th April 2000. 'A 1997 World Health Organisation report confirmed that cannabis has both acute and chronic health effects. The acute effects include damage to people's ability to learn and carry out many tasks, including operating machinery and driving vehicles. The chronic effects include damage to mental functioning, especially learning abilities, which may not be reversible for prolonged and heavy users... and the drug can exacerbate schizophrenia in people who are already affected by that illness. There are also obvious health risks associated with smoking the drug.'

But what the minister fails to discuss is how serious and widespread any of the risks he draws from the WHO report really are. A more recent, and at least as authoritative, analysis of the medical literature is contained in the 1998 Lancet review mentioned above. It concludes that 'on the medical evidence available, moderate indulgence in cannabis has little ill effect on health, and that decisions to ban or to legalise cannabis should be based on other considerations.'

It is worth taking in turn each point raised by the Minister to see how serious it is:

- 'the acute effects include damage to people's ability to... carry out many tasks, including... driving vehicles.'

The Lancet review of the literature concludes that cannabis has 'cognitive effects... that *may potentially* impair driving a motor vehicle'. It says that some laboratory studies suggest cannabis could have similar effects to alcohol. 'However, studies of the effects of cannabis on driving under more realistic conditions and on roads have shown much more modest impairments, probably because cannabis users are more aware of their impairment and less inclined to take risks than alcohol user... In two studies with a reasonable number of individuals (involved in actual road accidents) who had only used cannabis there was no clear evidence of increased culpability in these drivers...

so the main effect of cannabis use on driving may be in amplifying the impairments caused by alcohol, which is often used with the drug.'

However, this concern is easily addressed by levying penalties for driving under the influence of cannabis, and increasing the severity of penalties for driving after consuming both alcohol and cannabis.

- 'the chronic effects include damage to mental functioning...'

The Lancet review concludes that 'the long-term heavy use of cannabis does not produce the severe or grossly debilitating impairment of memory, attention, and cognitive function that is found with chronic heavy alcohol use.' However, 'studies show that it may produce more subtle impairments... it remains unclear how important they are for everyday functioning and whether they are reversed after an extended period of abstinence.'

- 'the drug can exacerbate schizophrenia...'

The Lancet review confirms that this is a plausible explanation but concludes that 'cannabis is unlikely to have caused cases of schizophrenia that would not otherwise have occurred'.

- 'there are also obvious health risks associated with smoking the drug.'

The Lancet review confirms this concern. Indeed there is some evidence that cannabis smoking may be even more likely than tobacco to generate bronchial ailments and to cause cancers especially if taken in conjunction with tobacco.

In short, although moderate and occasional cannabis use has few ill effects on health it can be harmful if used heavily over long periods. But unlike hard drugs 'no confirmed published cases world wide of human deaths from cannabis poisoning' exist. Its acute effects are less than those of alcohol and its chronic effects are not as serious as those of tobacco. Such health risks do not add up to a convincing case for prohibition on health grounds.

Nevertheless, anyone contemplating taking cannabis should be made aware of its health risks. The Lancet authors suggest that advice should be given about 'the possibility of being involved in a motor vehicle accident if patients drive while intoxicated by cannabis; the higher risk of an accident if they drive when intoxicated by both alcohol and cannabis; the respiratory risks of long-term cannabis smoking, which are substantially increased if they also smoke tobacco; and increased risk of developing dependence if they are daily users of cannabis; and the possibility of subtle cognitive impairment if they use regularly over several years.'

One of the consequences of criminalisation is that the authorities cannot ensure that such a health warning is displayed on its packaging.

(iii) 'Cannabis produces permanent behavioural consequences'

As with alcohol, most people consuming or intoxicated by the drug are likely to be somewhat relaxed and demotivated. Anyone taking cannabis (or alcohol) during working hours is likely to be ineffective at their job. But there is scant evidence that cannabis use permanently reduces people's drive and work ethic.

(iv) 'Cannabis leads to hard drug use'

Defenders of the current law against cannabis believe their strongest argument is that cannabis use leads to hard drug use. The theory is that cannabis is a 'gateway drug' that leads inexorably to the use of hard drugs.

This would indeed be a compelling argument for prohibition, but only if there were convincing evidence that taking cannabis does predispose people to go onto hard drugs who would not otherwise do so, and that prohibition of cannabis use stops people embarking on the first stage of this slippery slope.

In fact prohibition of cannabis use in this country has not stopped nearly half of young people trying cannabis (a higher proportion than in countries like Holland where it is not penalised). In any case, only one or two in every hundred people who use cannabis go onto try heroin. Anyone who is by personality, or because of social or other circumstances, predisposed to risk taking hard drugs will more than likely have tried less powerful drugs like cannabis *en route*. But these soft drugs do not cause the predisposition to try hard drugs. There is no known chemical factor which would make cannabis users more predisposed to try hard drugs, as the Lancet review confirms.

Although cannabis use of itself does not predispose people to try heroin, there are two ways in which the attempt to *prohibit* cannabis may actually increase the number of people who try hard drugs.

Demonising cannabis and equating it with hard drugs may have the perverse consequence of encouraging experimentation with hard drugs. Users who discover that cannabis has few of the ill effects claimed for it may be encouraged to try hard drugs too, on the assumption that their dangers are also exaggerated.

Secondly, if there is a link between cannabis and hard drug use, it is more likely to do with the fact that suppliers of cannabis also tend to be suppliers of hard drugs, which they may push to susceptible cannabis users. There is ample anecdotal evidence of this happening. But it is only because cannabis is illegal that it passes through the same illegal channels as hard drugs. The ability of legalisation to break this link is the most powerful argument in its favour.

(v) 'Cannabis use is immoral'
Many people instinctively feel that even if cannabis can be taken without risk to health or progressing to hard drugs it is still morally wrong. But many things that are contrary to the prevailing moral code are not crimes. Most people consider adultery to be wrong. But we do not fine or jail adulterers. It is bizarre to let people get drunk on alcohol (which is more likely than cannabis to lead to violence) but to criminalise them for smoking a single relaxing joint. A society with a better understanding of the moral law would be less inclined to resort to the criminal law to solve social problems.

The Dutch experience
Notwithstanding the fact that most countries are signatories of the 1961 single convention on drugs, there is a range of different approaches to tackling the drug issue. Britain tends to be at the most punitive end of the spectrum as far as cannabis is concerned. The United States – at least at the Federal level – also has one of the most punitive cannabis regimes. Yet both countries have among the highest levels of cannabis use.

The most frequently quoted country with a liberal approach is the Netherlands. In 1976, the Dutch decided to liberalise their law. The aim was to break the link between soft drug users and hard drug pushers, and to treat hard drug addiction as a medical rather than criminal problem. The use of cannabis and possession of cannabis for personal use were no longer penalised. To prevent cannabis users coming into contact with hard drug suppliers, the sale of cannabis in small quantities was permitted through licensed coffee shops. These outlets were not permitted to sell to people under 18 or to sell alcohol or hard drugs.

The Dutch policy of depenalising cannabis has now been running for nearly a quarter of a century. Technically, all trade in cannabis remains an administrative offence, but as a matter of declared policy the Dutch prosecutor will not prosecute for possession or sale in retail quantities or to licensed outlets.

As an experiment, it has been revealing in providing concrete evidence of the consequences of depenalisation. There are four measures by which we can evaluate the Dutch experiment in comparison with a more punitive approach:

(i) Has it reduced the level of hard drug use?

(ii) Has it resulted in wider use of cannabis itself?

(iii) Has it reduced crime?

(iv) Has it cut the costs of the criminal justice system?

On all four measures, the Dutch policy has much to recommend it.

(i) Has it reduced the level of hard drug use?

The main claim of those who support cannabis prohibition is that cannabis leads on to harder drugs. But the Dutch experiment has shown that it is not cannabis itself, but *cannabis prohibition*, that encourages the move to harder drugs. By providing legal outlets for cannabis, the Dutch have ensured that the cannabis user is no longer forced into the arms of the hard drug pusher. The following figure shows the levels of hard drug use across 14 European countries.

Figure 1   Levels of hard drug use in 14 European countries[150]

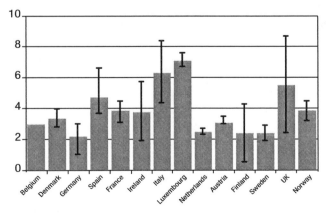

Range shows highest and lowest figures obtained by different methods

'Problem drug use' is defined here as 'intravenous or long-duration/regular use of opiates, cocaine and/or amphetamines'. This operational definition excludes Ecstasy and cannabis.

The table provides evidence that strongly supports the Dutch strategy. Despite its cannabis policy, there are substantially fewer heroin addicts per 100,000 of population in the Netherlands (160) than in the UK (260) or the USA (430). Moreover, the average age of Dutch addicts is rising, suggesting fewer young people are becoming addicted. The Dutch say that heroin addiction among teenagers is virtually unknown.[151] Only 1.8 per cent of young cannabis users in Holland have tried cocaine, whereas in the US the comparable figure is 16 per cent.

(ii) Has it resulted in wider use of cannabis itself?

Following liberalisation in 1976, cannabis usage did increase among Dutch youth. But usage also increased in most countries that continued to prohibit cannabis at the time. There is no evidence that cannabis use has increased due to depenalisation. Moreover it is remarkable that despite vigorous efforts to prohibit and discourage cannabis use in the UK we have the highest per capita usage in Europe – significantly higher than in Holland. And in the US, despite its 'war on drugs', cannabis usage is higher still.

Figure 2   Lifetime experience and last-twelve-months prevalence of cannabis use among adults in some EU countries and the US[152]

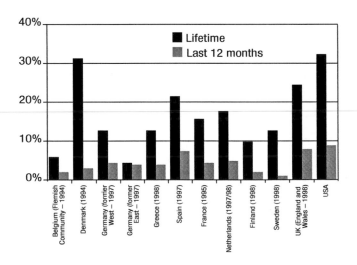

The most recent figures for all major legal and illegal drugs in the USA and Holland are as follows:

Table 1   Drug use among the population aged 12 and over in the United States and the Netherlands[153]

	Used once or twice		Used in the past year		Used in the past month	
	US	Neth'lands	US	Neth'lands	US	Neth'lands
Tobacco	70.5*	67.9	32.7*	38.1	29.6*	34.3
Cannabis	32.9	15.6	9.0	4.5	5.1	2.5
Volatile Substances	5.7	0.5	1.1	0.1	0.4	#
Alcohol	81.9	90.2	64.1	82.5	51.4	73.3
Heroin	0.9	0.3	0.3	0.1	#	#

* cigarettes only
# no figures available

One frequently cited consequence of Dutch policy is an alleged shift by Dutch users and suppliers to a stronger form of cannabis, with increased levels of THC (delta-nine-tetrahydro-cannibol), the active content of cannabis. But the true position is given by the respected Trimbos Institute. 'Various studies have shown that the percentages of THD in Nederweed can vary from 1.5 per cent to 13 per cent with peaks of up to 27 per cent. Similar to many kinds of imported cannabis, some variations of Nederweed (skunk) may contain high concentrations of THC, but this is not standard. In 1997 the Forensic Laboratory found an average THC level of 8.5 per cent in Dutch cannabis and 6 per cent in imported hemp.'

The evidence, too, is that users smoke smaller quantities of the stronger variant.

(iii) Has it reduced crime?

It is obvious that the Dutch policy of non-penalisation results in far fewer people being arrested or imprisoned for cannabis related offences. It has been claimed that the Dutch murder rate is disproportionately high and that this is related to drug use. The US Drug 'Czar', General Barry McCaffrey, gave this claim a high profile. However, it turned out that he was comparing the murder rate in the USA with a Dutch figure that included *attempted* murders. In fact, the Dutch murder rate is well below the US level, with 1.8 murders committed for every 100,000 compared with 8.2 murders in the U.S.

(iv) Has it cut the costs of the criminal justice system?

The Dutch taxpayer spends only a fraction of what his British and American equivalents spend on drug law enforcement.

Table 2   Per capita expenditure on drug law enforcement[154]

Holland	UK	USA
$7	$47	$110

The liberalising approach in the ascendant

A number of other countries have moved nearly as far as the Netherlands in depenalising cannabis use.

Following a court case which cast doubt on the constitutionality of criminalising cannabis, a number of German Länder no longer enforce the law against possession. Portugal and Switzerland have recently followed suite. Spain treats possession as an administrative rather than a criminal offence. Italy classifies supply of cannabis as an administrative offence subject to fine rather than imprisonment.

A number of US States have replaced criminal penalties with small civil fines for minor cannabis possession offences. This has had no apparent effect on cannabis use vis à vis neighbouring prohibitionist states and is popular with citizens. In 1998, the people of Oregon voted 2 to 1 against a proposal, adopted by their legislative leaders, to restore criminal sanctions.

Arguments and options for reforming the cannabis laws

The prohibition of cannabis use has been a failure. The law stands in need of reform. The main arguments for reforming the cannabis laws are clear.

- **It will break the link between soft and hard drugs**

This is the single most compelling prize to be won by changing our cannabis laws. It depends on making sufficiently radical changes to ensure that cannabis users are no longer brought into contact with the hard drug pushers.

- **It will restore respect for the law**

Because cannabis use is against the law, huge numbers of people find themselves flouting the law. According to BMA estimates, about 10 million people have done so – 4 million in the last year. Every year nearly 100,000 people are arrested for a cannabis related offence. Half are let off with a caution but have a criminal record as a result. All this contributes to the growing hostility to the law and its guardians across society in general, and among the young in particular. Cannabis users see in the law's differential treatment of cannabis, alcohol and nicotine nothing but a contemptible moral hypocrisy.

• It will liberate resources for dealing with hard drugs

Hard drugs are the main problem. They can kill, destroy people's lives and drive them to crime. But as over 80 per cent of all drug use relates to cannabis, most of the resources committed to the war against drugs are in fact absorbed in dealing with cannabis. Two-thirds of the arrests for drug related offences involve cannabis. Three-quarters of all drug seizures (by weight though not by value) involve cannabis. The cannabis tail is wagging the hard drug dog.

• It will encourage freedom and responsibility

A free society should demonstrate a bias against coercion. Wherever possible people should be allowed to make their own choices. People are more likely to behave responsibly the more responsibility they are allowed to exercise over their own lives. While there is a respectable case for the state trying to protect people from hard drugs, no such case is tenable in relation to cannabis.

Options for reform

In looking at how the law should be reformed, the overriding objective to bear in mind is the severing of the link between cannabis users and hard drug pushers. The present law forces cannabis users into contact with the criminals who supply both soft and hard drugs, with all the concomitant dangers that such contact brings.

Various options for reform exist, ranging from reducing the penalties for cannabis use, through decriminalisation, to total liberalisation. It is worth looking at them all in turn.

(i) Reducing penalties for possession for personal consumption

The Runciman Report for the Police Foundation recommended that possession of cannabis (and cultivation for personal use) should no longer be imprisonable offences. This would mean that they ceased to be arrestable offences in England and Wales (under section 24 of the Police and Criminal

Evidence Act). The Report went on to recommend that prosecution of offences for possession should be the exception. The norm would be a caution, which would no longer incur a criminal record.

This approach would reduce the friction between otherwise law abiding users of cannabis and the police. In particular, it would render unnecessary the greater part of the 300,000 stops and searches for drug offences (only 12 per cent of which result in finding drugs). It would also release substantial police and court resources.

However, cannabis users would still be lawbreakers. This would bring the law into contempt with the law-abiding majority, who feel that if something is a crime it should be punished. This approach also fails to achieve the prime purpose of reform – breaking the link between cannabis users and hard drug pushers. As long as trafficking in cannabis remains illegal it will tend to be handled by the same illegal channels that control heroin and crack.

(ii) Providing legal outlets

The whole logic of depenalisation, therefore, leads inexorably towards decriminalisation of possession for personal use. Short of legalising trade in cannabis entirely, the only way to stop driving soft drug users into the arms of the criminals who push hard drugs too, is to license some legal outlets to retail cannabis.

Holland's 'coffee shops' are the best example of legalised cannabis outlets, but it may not be desirable to copy them exactly. Moreover, they only count for half of all cannabis consumption, the other half still coming from criminal sources. A minimally effective approach to reform would be to legalise supply through outlets along the following lines:

Regulation of trade to protect against criminal elements
- Licensing justices would be given the task of licensing any outlets
- Justices would require licensees to be of good character
- Licences would be forfeited if anyone were convicted of supplying illegal drugs from the premises or if there were reasonable grounds for suspicion of such activities
- Tax would be levied on cannabis sales, set at a level which does not drive trade underground
- Buying or selling cannabis other than through licensed premises would remain a punishable offence

Discouraging promotion of cannabis use
- Only off-licences would be granted (there is no need to go as far as the Dutch by granting on-licences for consumption in 'coffee shops')
- The minimum age could be 18 (as for alcohol) rather than 16 (as is the case with tobacco)
- A maximum limit could be set on the amount sold to any individual
- Consumption of cannabis in public places could remain an offence
- Advertising and marketing should remain largely prohibited

Protection against health risks
- No alcohol could be sold from any premises licensed to sell cannabis
- Premises and products would be required to display full health warnings

(iii) Legalising cultivation of cannabis
The third step in liberalisation would be to legalise cultivation of cannabis in the UK for personal use and for wholesale trade. If possession for personal use were no longer a crime, it would be natural to permit cultivation for personal use. Once legal outlets are licensed they will need a steady source of supplies. To go further and permit cultivation to supply licensed outlets would have the benefit of creating an entirely legal supply chain. To the extent that supplies become available, UK licensed outlets would then not need to obtain supplies from the international criminal gangs who often handle hard drugs as well.

(iv) Full legalisation
The series of options outlined so far still falls far short of the full legalisation advocated by some on libertarian grounds. There is much to be said for a cautious step by step approach here as in most areas of social policy. Moreover, the intention of reform is not to endorse cannabis use still less to encourage its abuse. A strict regulatory regime will reflect public concern that if people use cannabis at all they should do so responsibly.

Conclusion
The legislation suggested by options i), ii) and iii) would be consistent with the UK's international treaty obligations. The 1961 UN Single Convention on Narcotic Drugs is somewhat ambiguous in its wording. It requires signatories to control rather than prohibit trade in cannabis. It is likely that the reforms envisaged above are compatible with the Convention.

This framework is the minimal coherent strategy that can be adopted which actually fulfils the purpose of insulating cannabis users from peddlers of hard drugs and other criminal elements. It would re-establish respect for the law while preserving individuals' freedom and responsibility. And it would leave governments in a better position to tackle the problems of hard drug use and serious crime.

8. SUPPLY REDUCTION: WHY IT DOESN'T WORK

Donald McCarthy

In 2001-2002, the British government plans to spend £373 million on measures designed to raise the street price of illegal drugs. This is the largest single item in the national drugs budget, accounting for 43 per cent of the total. This figure is planned to increase over the next three years. Yet despite this massive expenditure, the price of heroin and cocaine in Britain continues to fall. This essay seeks to provide an explanation for this apparent puzzle.

To begin with, we must try to gain a clearer understanding of the phenomenon of addiction. Popular discussion of illegal drugs rests on a crude notion of addiction. Addiction is thought of as an uncontrollable craving that has to be satisfied at any cost – to health, family, career, life itself. The only way the state can protect citizens against the danger of addiction is by cutting off the supply of addictive drugs completely, making their use impossible.

To people who hold this view, the idea of regulating the use of addictive drugs by manipulating their price seems absurd. The point about addiction is that it is 'uncontrollable', and therefore insensitive to changes in price. If the street price of heroin goes up, addicts will just steal more and more goods from other people to satisfy their craving.

This crude view of addiction is not held by the law enforcement agencies. The main object of those whose job it is to interdict the supply of illegal drugs is to reduce consumption by forcing up their selling price. They act on the assumption that the more costly it is to obtain the drug, the less of it will be used. They think, that is, like economists, treating drugs like apples or any other familiar object of desire.

These policies are logical and coherent. Their only problem is that they don't seem to work. Drug agencies worldwide constantly report great victories in the 'war against drugs', but the street price of most drugs continues to fall. This essay shows why. It analyses the use of addictive drugs like cocaine and heroin using models of demand and supply developed by economists to deal with the particular characteristics of this kind of good. It supports the analysis with the data – mainly from the United States – on drug production and sale. This data is admittedly sketchy; the trade in these illegal substances cannot be accurately recorded. The conclusion is that the 'war on drugs' is not being won, and the prospects for 'winning' it are poor. What should replace it is left open.

PART I
The Demand for Addictive Drugs

A discipline such as economics, concerned as it is with the optimising behaviour of rational individuals, seems to have little of value to bring to the study of addiction. Addicts are commonly seen as slaves to the substance they abuse, incapable of resisting the temptation to 'hit' no matter how high the price in lost income or impaired health.

But although its methodology appears unpromising, economics can improve our understanding of why individuals begin and maintain addictions and the effects that changes in the cost (both monetary and medical) of addictive drugs have on their consumption.

The Becker-Murphy Model: Rational Addiction
The most influential and best-known model of demand for addictive substances is that devised by Gary Becker and Kevin Murphy.[155] The Becker-Murphy model is generally referred to as a model of 'rational addiction'. This should not be understood to imply that addicts are rational in the common sense of that term; addicts are rational only in the technical sense that they engage in 'forward looking maximization with stable preferences'. Addiction is rational insofar as it realises the addict's particular goals; whether or not those goals themselves are rational is a question on which economics has nothing to say.

Individuals in the Becker-Murphy model act 'as though' they maximised a fairly simple utility function.[156] The utility – or pleasure – derived from a shot of an addictive drug depends on two things. The first is the drug itself; the second is the individual's past consumption of the drug. This last is called the individual's 'consumption capital' and is designed to capture the notion of addiction. Consumption capital is said to be reinforcing. The more one consumes now, other things being equal, the more one will want to consume in the future. This is consistent with what we know about the addictive nature of cigarettes, heroin and rock cocaine. The second feature is that current consumption lowers the future utility derived from taking the drug. This is what is commonly known as the tolerance effect. Every unit of the drug consumed gives less pleasure than the last unit; one has to take more to get the same effect. Again, this is wholly consistent with what we know about addiction.

The Becker-Murphy model also assumes that consumers of drugs – like consumers generally – attach more value to present benefits than to future benefits. They 'discount' the future. This discount factor is assumed to vary between individuals and groups. Individuals who discount the future heavily are more likely to be consumers of addictive drugs (and therefore more likely to be addicts) than more future-oriented individuals. This can be understood if one considers the cost of taking drugs. This cost has two parts. The first is the money cost of the substance consumed – the price of the drug per unit times the number of units purchased. The second part is the present value of the future adverse effects of current consumption. These adverse effects include lower earnings and impaired health. The more heavily the individual discounts the future, the smaller the present value of these costs will be. Addictive drugs are thus comparatively cheaper for present-oriented individuals than for future-oriented individuals.

It has often been observed that the poor tend to discount the future more heavily than the better off. We can therefore predict that the poor will find addictive substances more attractive than the rich. This prediction does indeed seem to be born out by the facts. This has worrying implications for those who favour decriminalisation or legalisation of addictive drugs. As the second section of this essay will make explicit, the price of illegal drugs is positively related to the fact that they are illegal, to the amount of enforcement applied by authorities and to the penalties imposed upon apprehended producers, traffickers and dealers. Legalisation – or less dramatically decriminalisation – of a certain drug will immediately cause its price to fall. If this policy were accompanied by an education programme designed to make the future costs of drug consumption more apparent, the net effect would be to reduce the increase in drug consumption much more amongst wealthy than amongst poorer consumers.

The other noteworthy conclusion of the model is that there is no reason to believe that the demand for illegal drugs is unresponsive to changes either in the money price of drugs or in the future adverse consequences of their use. On the contrary, there are good reasons to suppose that demand will in fact be responsive to both sets of changes. This conclusion seems to be well born out by the data on the price-elasticity of heroin and cocaine displayed below.

The O'Donoghue-Rabin model: Irrational Addiction

The Becker-Murphy model assumes that drug users discount the future at a uniform rate. It assumes that they value jam tomorrow less than jam today, and jam the day-after-tomorrow by *as much less* again. Their preferences are – in the jargon – 'time-consistent'. This assumption does not square with what we take to be true of human beings in general and drug addicts in particular. Drug addicts are normally thought to be weak-willed people, incapable of forgoing any opportunity for immediate gratification. Their preferences are thought to be 'time-inconsistent'. Ted O'Donoghue and Matthew Rabin have revised the Becker-Murphy model so as to incorporate this assumption.[157]

What is meant by time-inconsistency? It is not the same thing as discounting the future. It is quite possible to discount the future while at the same time having time-consistent preferences. A person with time-inconsistent preferences not only discounts the future; he discounts the future at an *inconsistent* rate. Offered the choice between utility at a later date and utility at an earlier date, such a person's relative preference for earlier over the later utility *increases* as the earlier date gets closer. The person with time-inconsistent preferences is, in short, impatient; he has a 'tendency to pursue immediate gratification'.

Like Becker and Murphy, O'Donoghue and Rabin assume that individuals are forward-looking maximisers, and so take into account both present and future costs of drug use. They assume that the individual takes a 'hit' of the drug if the benefit of doing so outweighs the present costs and the present value of future costs. However, individuals in the O'Donoghue-Rabin model have time-inconsistent preferences. They are therefore likely always to overestimate their ability to resist temptation in the future, because the benefits of a hit acquire a higher value relative to its subsequent costs the closer it moves towards the present. (For those with time-consistent preferences, on the other hand, the ratio remains constant.) People with time-inconsistent preferences are particularly vulnerable to addiction, because they systematically overestimate their ability to quit.

One advantage of the O'Donoghue-Rabin model over the Becker-Murphy model is that it explains the greater vulnerability of the young to addiction. It is a commonplace that young people have a greater tendency 'to pursue immediate gratification' – which is another way of saying that they have time-inconsistent preferences. This being the case, the O'Donoghue-Rabin model would predict that they have a greater tendency to become hooked on addictive drugs. And this is indeed born out by the facts; there are very few heroin and cocaine addicts over fifty. The O'Donoghue-Rabin model also captures our intuitive belief that addicts frustrate their own long-term interests, whereas the Becker-Murphy model cannot make sense of this idea. It is, in short, a model not of rational but of *irrational* addiction.

The effects of price on demand

In spite of their differences, both models examined above agree in one crucial respect. They both assume that the greater the cost of drug use, the less people will indulge in it. Drugs, in short, are not exempt from the usual economic laws governing demand.

These assumptions are supported by the facts. A fair amount of empirical work has been done in an attempt to estimate the impact of a change in price – temporary or permanent – on consumption. These studies of the 'price elasticity of demand' have typically not been informed by a formal model of addiction. Nonetheless, they appear to confirm some of the conclusions of the work of Becker, Murphy, O'Donoghue and Rabin. It has sometimes been assumed that the price elasticity of demand for illicit drugs by addicts is inelastic. This is intuitively appealing; popular literature and the media portray addicts as 'hopped up' junkies willing to pay *any* price no matter *how* high. But such stereotypes are not supported by the available data. Using data on pre-World War II opium consumption in present-day Indonesia, Jan van Ours estimates a short-run elasticity of demand of -0.7 and a long run elasticity of -1.0.[158] Howard Saffer and Frank Chaloupka put the price elasticity for heroin at between -1.8 to -1.6, and for cocaine between -1.1 to -0.66.[159] Jonathan Caulkins estimates the elasticity of demand for cocaine as being between -1.5 and -2.0.[160] These are not particularly small estimates. For cocaine, an increase of 1 per cent in price will decrease use by between 1.35 per cent and 2 per cent, while for heroin a 1 per cent increase in price is associated with a fall in use of between 1 per cent and 1.8 per cent. The price elasticity of demand for heroin and cocaine is, according to many estimates, greater than it is for cigarettes.

The policy implications of these studies are obvious. Contrary to popular belief, an increase in the price of heroin or rock cocaine will not simply result in more crime by addicts and no reduction in use. The sensitivity of users' demand to even relatively small increases in price is much greater than one might think. This suggests that efforts to discourage use by raising price can in principle succeed. Supply side measures cannot be dismissed *a priori*. However, as I hope to show in the next part of this essay, there are good reasons for thinking that they do not work in practice.

Part II

The Supply of Addictive Drugs

Attempts to suppress the supply of illegal drugs divide into three main categories. First of all, there is the attempt to suppress production at source, by means of either crop substitution programmes or outright destruction of crops. Secondly, there is the attempt to interdict drugs as they come into the country. Third, there is the attempt to deter drug dealers within the country by means of criminal penalties. The aim of all three measures is, of course, to push up the street price of drugs and thereby reduce consumption.

Most of the detailed economic research on the relative efficiency of different supply-side measures comes from the United State. This research relies on data that is, in the nature of things, of poor quality. The drug industry, being illegal, is inherently opaque. Estimates of drug production by the United Nations, and the more authoritative estimates published annually in the 'International Narcotics Control Strategy Report', are remarkably inconsistent over time and often implausibly large.[161] Additionally, the methodologies used to generate these estimates are inadequately described and apparently subject to unexpected revision. However, although one must be cautious in drawing any conclusions from such sketchy data, it does provide broad lessons about the relative efficacy of different supply-side policies.

(A) Production Suppression

The main internationally traded drugs are cocaine and heroin. Both are partially refined agricultural commodities – cocaine is a product of coca leaves and heroin is a product of opium poppies. Coca bushes are grown in significant quantity in just three South American countries: Bolivia, Colombia and Peru, with Bolivia and Peru producing a superior product in terms of alkaloid content. Opium poppies are more widely cultivated and heroin produced in a greater number of countries. Mexico, Colombia, Laos, Vietnam, Thailand, Pakistan, Burma and Afghanistan all produce opium gum – the raw product from which heroin is derived. Production, however, is concentrated in just two countries – Burma and Afghanistan – which together account for between 90 per cent[162] and 94 per cent[163] of all the heroin produced in the world.

The production of hashish, powder cocaine and heroin has many affinities with the processing of agricultural commodities in general, the main differences relating to the need to minimise the risk of product seizure – and thus to minimize plant size – and the relatively low importance of research and development. These considerations encourage relatively small-scale and surprisingly labour-intensive manufacturing facilities (and indeed, in Mexico, small scale crop production) and less bulky, increasingly potent products. A good example of this second phenomenon is found in cannabis, the most bulky of all illicit drugs, where TCH content has risen sharply over the last 30 years. It can be observed to a lesser extent in cocaine, where Colombian coca potency is rising.[164]

Capital plays an unimportant role in the production of illicit drugs – labour and raw materials are the only really important inputs into the productive process. The costs of raw materials and labour are low. Jonathan Caulkins and Peter Reuter estimate that the wholesale price of cocaine and heroin at source is about 1 per cent of US retail prices.[165] A kilogram of cocaine in Colombia costs only between $800 and $1,600, and a kilogram of heroin in Bangkok costs around $7,000 to $11,000. If producers are 'price takers' in illicit drugs wholesale markets – and this seems reasonable given that criminal cartels are not very effective in manipulating price – then the wages of workers in the cocaine or heroin industries are proportional to the export price of the drug. And if labour markets are efficient, then wages in the narcotics sector cannot rise permanently above wages in the non-drugs sector.[166] As the price of heroin or cocaine rises, legitimately employed workers (mostly farmers) enter the illegal drugs industry, thereby pushing wages down. There is anecdotal evidence to suggest that in South America wages are higher in the cocaine sector but there exists no statistical proof of this supposition, and it is likely that any difference can be accounted for by the premia required to compensate workers for risk.

An understanding of the basic economics of cocaine and heroin production is crucial to policymakers, given the huge sums of money expended on crop-substitution and crop-destruction programmes. The efficacy of such programmes, which essentially attempt to increase the costs and risks of drug production, depends crucially on the nature of the industry. David Kennedy, Peter Reuter and Kevin Jack Riley provide a calibrated general equilibrium model of the cocaine market in the three Andean cocaine producers.[168] While the model does not provide a detailed formal analysis of the distribution, wholesaling and retailing industries, it provides a rich enough environment to test the efficacy of certain supply-side policies under certain assumptions.

Coca refining is a simple vertical process, in which cocaine is produced sequentially from a series of intermediate products: coca leaves, then coca paste and then cocaine base. The inputs into cocaine manufacture are these raw materials and labour – capital isn't explicitly modelled. The production of other GDP products is represented by a standard[167] production function with labour and capital as inputs. Total employment in the economies modelled is assumed to be exogenous and labour is paid its marginal product. The export price of cocaine is a weighted average of internal prices in Peru, Bolivia and Colombia[169] and the 'law of one price' is achieved not through arbitrage but rather through internal non-market mechanisms in the cocaine industry. The demand for cocaine exports is a function of the world price of the drug. The world price of cocaine is the sum of the export price plus an exogenous mark-up (a key assumption, as will be made explicit later), so exporters capture the rents comprised by the fact that a no-arbitrage condition is assumed not to hold across the three Andean producers. The use of a fixed mark-up is justified by the assumption that the mark-up – the rewards to all those agents further down the supply chain (shippers, distributors, wholesalers and dealers) – is related to the *quantity* of cocaine sold and not its *value*.

One of the most popular techniques of production suppression is crop-substitution. The aim of crop-substitution – recently affirmed as an important plank of the United Nations' anti-drug misuse strategy and now operative in many countries – is to provide the suppliers of the most basic raw materials of drug production (here coca leaves) with more profitable legal economic opportunities. The idea is that if other economic alternatives can be made more attractive to farmers, they will choose not to supply coca paste refiners with leaves. Cocaine manufacturers' costs will rise, as they are forced to increase their bid-price for coca. This increase in the cost of coca will then be transmitted to the distributor in the form of higher cocaine prices and finally to the consumer. Since the demand for drugs appears to be price elastic, as demonstrated above, consumers will buy fewer drugs and many users will stop consuming altogether.

Kennedy *et. al.* examine the effect of crop-substitution (and economic aid programmes in general) on production and prices by modelling the impact of an increase in capital stock in Peru and Bolivia, using 1989 data. An increase in capital investment raises the marginal product of labour and – since it is assumed that labour is paid its marginal product – the wages paid to workers in the non-cocaine sector. As workers are drawn into the non-cocaine sector, the cocaine industry must pay them more to lure them back. So far so good. However, since labour-costs comprise a tiny proportion of the world cocaine price, and an even smaller proportion of its wholesale and retail price, any increases here will have a minute effect on the street price of cocaine. Indeed, changes in price caused by crop substitution are 'so trivial that there is a negligible change in the level of consumption'.[170] This is illustrated by the table below.

Table 1   The effect of an increase in capital stock on the user retail price of cocaine[171]

	Peru and Bolivia				World Cocaine Market		
Capital Stock ($ bns)	Wage ($)	Final Non-cocaine GDP ($ bns)	Non-cocaine GDP Labour (millions)	Cocaine Product Labour (millions)	Output (metric tons)	Export Price ($1,000 per kg)	User Retail Price ($1,000 per kg)
60	840	28.40	11.60	0.74	736.37	3.82	135.00
70	940	31.60	11.60	0.74	736.14	3.90	135.08
80	1030	34.70	11.60	0.74	735.93	3.98	135.16
90	1110	37.60	11.60	0.74	735.73	4.05	135.24
100	1190	40.50	11.60	0.74	735.53	4.13	135.31
110	1270	43.20	11.60	0.74	735.34	4.20	135.38
120	1350	45.80	11.60	0.74	735.16	4.26	135.45

The table shows the impact of a programme designed to expand the capital stock of Peru and Bolivia from its 1989 level of $60 billion. Doubling the capital stock to $120 billion has the effect of increasing wages in those countries by some 60 per cent. However, it has only a small impact on world cocaine output and an infinitesimal effect on retail prices. Assuming a conservative price elasticity of demand of -1.5, doubling the capital stock of

Peru and Bolivia would reduce world demand for cocaine by just 0.5 per cent. This is represented visually in the graph below.

Figure 1   The effect of an increase in capital stock on the user retail price of cocaine

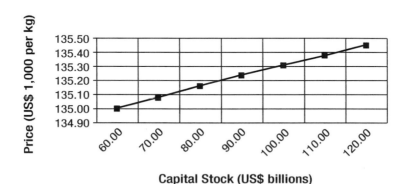

Capital Stock (US$ billions)

The other widespread method of production suppression is crop and facility destruction. This is a mainstay of Mexican anti-drug operations. It is also practiced to some extent in Colombia (where the aerial spraying of herbicides is permitted) and to a far lesser extent in Peru and Bolivia. Like crop-substitution schemes, the destruction of drugs during the production stage is designed to raise the costs of producing drugs and thus wholesale prices.

However, like crop-substitution, crop-destruction does not appear to be a particularly efficient way of increasing user retail prices. As the following table shows, destruction rates of 30 per cent (around the proportion currently estimated to be destroyed by Government programmes in the Andean producing countries) increase the export price per kilogram by some 13 per cent and retail prices by just 0.4 per cent.

Destruction programmes only begin to effect prices when the fraction of production destroyed becomes very high. The marginal impact of every extra percentage of cocaine destroyed is very small until the destruction rate reaches 90 per cent. Such a high destruction rate is unlikely to be realised, given the incentives it would provide to decentralise production (as has occurred in Mexico). It would also be strongly resisted by the governments of Peru and Bolivia.

Table 2   The effect of crop destruction on the user retail price of cocaine[172]

Peru, Bolivia and Colombia				World Cocaine Market		
Fraction of Cocaine destroyed	Wage ($)	Final Non-cocaine GDP ($ bns)	Non-cocaine GDP Labour (millions)	Cocaine Product Labour (millions)	Output (metric tons)	Export Price ($1,000 per kg)	User Retail Price ($1,000 per kg)
0.00	1070.00	60.40	23.30	0.96	736.37	3.82	135.00
0.10	1080.00	60.30	23.20	1.07	736.00	3.95	135.13
0.30	1080.00	60.00	22.90	1.38	734.94	4.34	135.53
0.50	1100.00	59.50	22.40	1.92	732.94	5.08	136.26
0.70	1140.00	58.30	21.10	3.18	727.80	7.02	138.20
0.90	1530.00	51.20	15.20	9.05	687.62	23.64	154.82
0.95	2600.00	38.60	8.40	15.94	598.97	72.86	204.04

Figure 2   The effect of crop-destruction on the user retail price of cocaine

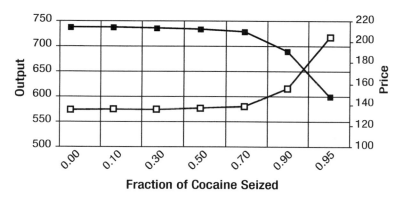

—■— Output (metric tons)   —□— User Retail Price (1,000 US$ per kg)

The central assumption underpinning these results is that of a fixed mark-up. This is the assumption that the economic reward accruing to agents involved in the cocaine industry is proportional to the quantity of cocaine sold rather than to its price. The fixed mark-up assumption implies an 'additive' price transmission mechanism.[173] In other words, increasing the wholesale price of cocaine by $1 per kilogram will increase its retail price by $1 per kilogram. Given that the retail price of cocaine is vastly greater than its wholesale price, however, this represents a huge proportional decrease. However, if reward is proportional to price rather than quantity, a 1 per cent increase in wholesale prices will increase retail prices by 1 per cent. If this 'multiplicative' model is a better approximation to reality, then the effects of enforcement programmes are dramatically improved. The different results obtained under the two assumptions are shown in the tables below.

Table 3   The effect of an increase in capital stock on the user retail price of cocaine according to both additive and multiplicative models[174]

			Peru, Bolivia and Colombia			World Cocaine Market		
Capital Stock	Wage ($)	Final Non- cocaine GDP ($ bns)	Non- cocaine GDP Labour (millions)	Cocaine Product Labour (millions)	Output (metric tons)	Export Price ($1,000 per kg)	User Retail Price ($1,000 per kg) Additive Model	User Retail Price ($1,000 per kg) Multi- plicative Model
60.00	840.00	28.40	11.60	0.74	736.37	3.82	135.00	135.00
70.00	940.00	31.60	11.60	0.74	736.14	3.90	135.08	137.83
80.00	1030.00	34.70	11.60	0.74	735.93	3.98	135.16	140.74
90.00	1110.00	37.60	11.60	0.74	735.73	4.05	135.24	143.30
100.00	1190.00	40.50	11.60	0.74	735.53	4.13	135.31	146.21
110.00	1270.00	43.20	11.60	0.74	735.34	4.20	135.38	148.77
120.00	1350.00	45.80	11.60	0.74	735.16	4.26	135.45	150.97

Table 4   The effect of crop-destruction on the user retail price of cocaine according to both additive and multiplicative models[175]

			Peru, Bolivia and Colombia			World Cocaine Market		
Fraction of cocaine destroyed	Wage ($)	Final Non- cocaine GDP ($ bns)	Non- cocaine GDP Labour (millions)	Cocaine Product Labour (millions)	Output (metric tons)	Export Price ($1,000 per kg)	User Retail Price ($1,000 per kg) Additive Model	User Retail Price ($1,000 per kg) Multi- plicative Model
0.00	1070.00	60.40	23.30	0.96	736.37	3.82	135.00	135.00
0.10	1080.00	60.30	23.20	1.07	736.00	3.95	135.13	139.59
0.30	1080.00	60.00	22.90	1.38	734.94	4.34	135.53	153.52
0.50	1100.00	59.50	22.40	1.92	732.94	5.08	136.26	180.23
0.70	1140.00	58.30	21.10	3.18	727.80	7.02	138.20	250.40
0.90	1530.00	51.20	15.20	9.05	687.62	23.64	154.82	855.25
0.95	2600.00	38.60	8.40	15.94	598.97	72.86	204.04	2952.93

Comparing the two right hand columns in both tables shows that if rewards are proportional to the value rather than the quantity of the product, then the effects of enforcement will be much greater. This is demonstrated dramatically in the following charts.

Figure 3   The effect of an increase in capital stock on the user retail price of cocaine according to both additive and multiplicative models

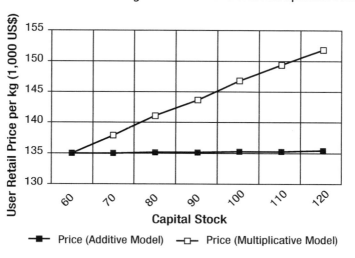

Figure 4   The effect of crop-destruction on the user retail price of cocaine according to both additive and multiplicative models

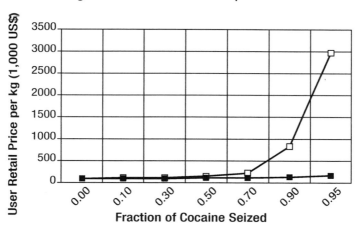

While there is evidence that the multiplicative model may be more consistent with the data than the additive model,[176] the choice of model depends on what end of the drug distribution chain one is studying. At the coca growing and paste-refining end, variations in coca leaf prices unparalleled by retail prices and perhaps the lower importance of retaining staff loyalty would make the additive model more appropriate. Further down the distribution chain, where the need to maintain gang cohesiveness may be much more important (and this cost element is proportional to price rather than quantity) a multiplicative model seems more appropriate. This has clear policy implications. Policies aiming to increase costs at the higher end of the distribution chain are the *least* efficient, since it is to this end of the chain that the additive model applies. Efforts would be better focused on the lower end of the chain, since it is here that every additional rise in cost can be expected to have a *proportional* effect on retail price.

(B) Interdiction

Three illicit drugs comprise the bulk of the international drugs trade: cannabis, heroin and cocaine. With the exception of Ecstasy, synthetics are generally produced close to or within the country of consumption.[177] We will concentrate here on cocaine and heroin.

Cocaine trade and distribution

Much of the international trade in cocaine was formerly controlled by a Colombian duopoly comprising the Medellin and Cali cartels. The importance of these large organisations has, due to extensive US and Colombian law-enforcement activities, declined and in their place smaller scale operators from the Northern Valle del Cauca have come to prominence.[178] Often employing citizens of the Dominican Republic as franchisees on the East Coast of the US, these Colombian firms now appear to control the vast majority of cocaine traffic in the US. Columbians also work in association with a number of Mexican criminal groups, who are responsible for smuggling some two-thirds of US cocaine imports over the Mexican border.

The trans-Atlantic cocaine trade is also a focus for the Colombian successors to the Medellin and Cali organisations. Traffickers based in Northern Valle del Cauca run much of the Colombian-European cocaine trade as a joint venture with Spanish criminal organisations based in Galicia. The Colombian gangs ship cocaine from Colombia and the other Andean producers to Central

America and the Caribbean where the Galicians pick it up and transport it across the Atlantic, chiefly to the rocky coast of Galicia. It is estimated that 'Spain is a chief, and possibly the chief, gateway for cocaine shipments into Europe'.[179] Cocaine from Colombia (some of it Bolivian and Peruvian re-exports) is also shipped to Europe via Africa. Nigerian organisations, which are also key traffickers of non-South American heroin to the US, have turned Nigeria into a major heroin and cocaine transport hub. Cocaine is also imported into Europe via South Africa.

Cocaine trafficking and distribution in Europe lacks the same level of organisation as North American market.[180] Distributors in the UK tend to be criminals running a number of other illegal enterprises. However, there is some evidence that the European cocaine market is consolidating. In addition to the Colombian-Galician partnership, there appear to be growing linkages between Colombian producers and Italian and Russian organised crime.

Heroin trade and distribution

Four regions export heroin to the US: Mexico, Colombia, South West Asia and the 'Golden Triangle' in South East Asia. Key importation points are California, Florida, New York and Texas. The great bulk of Mexican heroin is imported via California; Colombian heroin is divided between Florida and New York, and Asian heroin is imported largely via New York.[181]

The European market has traditionally been controlled by Turkish and ethnic Turkish criminals, who traffic heroin into Europe along the 'Balkan Route'. The source of the bulk of these imports is Afghanistan, which is a large importer of acetic anhydride – one of heroin's key precursor chemicals. Afghani heroin is transported through Pakistan, Iran and Turkey. It then enters Europe, where the Balkan Route divides. The northern route runs through Romania, Hungary and on to Northern Europe. The southern route, which supplies Western Europe, runs via the Former Yugoslav republics (where the Albanian-separatist KLA is an important trafficker), Greece and increasingly Albania. Heroin is typically smuggled along the Balkan Route concealed in trans-international route trucks, which are subject to inspection only at source and destination.

Distribution of Balkan Route heroin is usually undertaken by Turks based within the primary countries of consumption. In the United Kingdom, most available heroin is imported by sea and distributed by Turkish organisations based in north London and Liverpool. London-based gangs supply the south of England and the Midlands while the Liverpool organisations supply the drug to Glasgow and Edinburgh, Dublin, Manchester and the rest of Northwest England.

Other routes of export for Afghani heroin to Europe run through the former Soviet Central Asian Republics, through Nigeria and through Pakistan. Pakistan is becoming an increasingly important point of departure for UK heroin imports. Airline passengers from Pakistan carry small consignments of southwest Asian heroin, which are then distributed by ethnic Pakistani criminal organisations in Britain.

The costs of interdiction

Disrupting the transport of illicit drugs is one of the major strategies employed by the international law enforcement community. As with crop substitution and destruction, the logic underlying the interdiction of drug shipments is to increase the wholesale and retail price of drugs and thus cut consumption. The US alone spends around $2,000 million on interdiction efforts every year. These expenditures represent over a tenth of total US governmental anti-drugs spending and between a seventh and a fifth of US spending on supply reduction programmes. Europe, the second largest retail market for most illicit drugs, also has interdiction at the heart of its anti-drugs strategy, with seizures of the three main trafficked drugs high and rising.

British policy is no exception to the rule. Reducing the availability of drugs is one of the four goals of the government's 10-year plan and the UK Anti-Drugs Co-ordinator has set targets to reduce the availability of Class A drugs (including cocaine, heroin and Ecstasy) by 25 per cent by 2005 and by 50 per cent by 2008. Keith Hellawell has remarked: 'we are focusing our efforts where they can have most impact – further up the supply chain. We are disrupting more class A drug traffickers and increasing the assets seized from traffickers.'[182]

The government's Comprehensive Spending Review 2000 makes a total of nearly 700 million pounds available for combating drug misuse. Of this total, a large proportion is to be allocated to reducing availability – presumably focusing on the upper end of the drug supply chain. Until 2002-03, availability reduction is planned to remain the single largest constituent part of the cross-departmental drugs programme.

Table 5   Projected interdepartmental expenditure on UK drug policy measures, in pounds sterling[183]

| | Strategy Area | | | | |
Year	Drug treatment	Protecting young people	Safeguarding communities	Reducing availability	Total
2000-01	234	63	45	353	695
2001-02	328	90	79	373	870
2002-03	377	97	81	376	931
2003-04	401	120	95	380	996

Table 6   Projected interdepartmental expenditure on UK drug policy measures, as a percentage of the total

| | Strategy Area | | | | |
Year	Drug treatment	Protecting young people	Safeguarding communities	Reducing availability	Total
2000-01	34%	9%	6%	51%	100%
2001-02	38%	10%	9%	43%	100%
2002-03	40%	10%	9%	40%	100%
2003-04	40%	12%	10%	38%	100%

The determination to interrupt the drug trade is reflected in the impressive seizure records of HM Customs and Excise and the UK's police forces.

Figure 5   UK seizures of heroin[184]

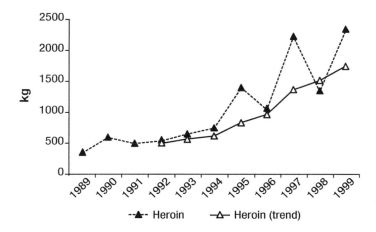

Figure 6   UK seizures of cocaine[185]

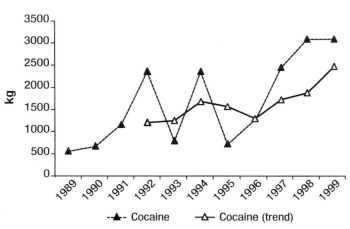

The efficacy of interdiction programmes

But these heroic efforts seem at first sight to have had no effect whatsoever on the retail price of heroin and cocaine. Interdiction programmes appear to be a striking failure and the funds supporting them a waste of taxpayers' money. This is certainly the implication of the following chart:

Figure 7   Seizures as a percentage of cocaine smuggled into the US compared with cocaine retail price[186]

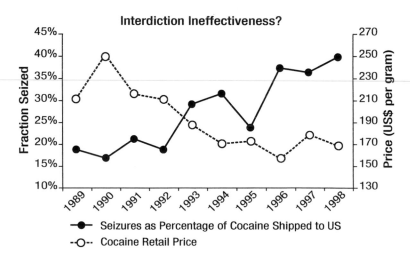

Between 1989 and 1998, seizures of cocaine as a proportion of shipments to the US have risen, while the retail price of powder cocaine has fallen. (Clearly, the seizure percentage here is little more than a guess.) These are exactly the reverse of the figures one might expect from a successful seizures policy. How are they to be explained?

Jonathan Caulkins, Gordon Crawford and Peter Reuter try to model the effects of cocaine interdiction on US retail price.[187] The cost of smuggling cocaine is equal to the physical costs of transport, the risk-premium paid to the smugglers, and the cost of replacing interdicted cargos. Intensifying interdiction raises the cost of smuggling by increasing both the number of lost cargos and the risk-premium paid to smugglers. But a crucial assumption of the model is that traffickers can respond to the efforts of the interdiction community by altering their smuggling method and their selected route of trade. The model assumes the existence of three different smuggling methods and a number of different routes. Cocaine can be imported into the US by five air-routes, five sea-routes, and finally by land – a 'backstop' route that is relatively immune to increased interdiction efforts.

The existence of such a backstop route has important implications for interdiction. If it is possible for smugglers to switch to a method of transport that is relatively impervious to law enforcement, then interdiction yields diminishing marginal returns. The marginal effect of an increase in interdiction eventually becomes negligible. This means that its effect in raising the retail price and thus reducing the consumption of the drug is negligible too.

It makes a crucial difference too whether the additive or the multiplicative model holds. If price increases are transmitted by an additive process – as is implied by a fixed mark-up – then even an interdiction programme that doubled the frequency of seizure on all routes would have only a marginal impact on consumption. Even if the multiplicative model of transmission is a better approximation of reality, seizure programmes that double the interdiction rate must apply to at least 80 per cent of shipment routes to have a marked impact on usage. Another unpleasant lesson can also be drawn from Caulkins et al. If the fixed mark-up hypothesis is an accurate one, increasing interdiction activities can have the perverse effect of *raising* the value of the drug. This can be seen in the third column of Table 7, represented graphically in Figure 9. A programme that doubles the likelihood of interdiction on all routes reduces domestic consumption by 40 metric tons, but also increases the value of cocaine exports from $1180 million to $1650 million. This would of course increase the rewards of trafficking, thereby stimulating further supply. Interdiction can, in short, shoot itself in the foot.

Table 7   The effect of doubling the interdiction rate along various smuggling routes[188]

Number of Air and Sea Routes Affected	Elasticity of Retail Price with Respect to the Import Price = 0.2 (Additive Markup)		Elasticity of Retail Price with Respect to the Import Price = 0.9 (Multiplicative Markup)	
	Amount Delivered (metric tons)	Export Value ($ billions)	Amount Delivered (metric tons)	Export Value ($ billions)
0&0	300	1180	300	1180
1&0	299	1190	297	1170
1&1	297	1220	290	1160
2&1	296	1230	283	1140
2&2	294	1260	276	1120
3&2	290	1300	264	1080
3&3	287	1340	253	1040
4&3	284	1390	240	960
4&4	278	1450	223	860
5&4	271	1540	192	770
5&5	260	1650	155	590

Figure 8   The effect of doubling the interdiction rate along various smuggling routes on quantity of cocaine imported

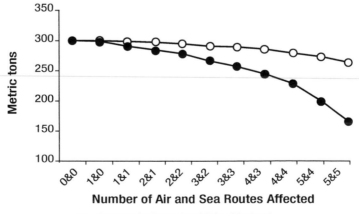

-O- Amount Delivered (Additive Markup)
-●- Amount Delivered (Multiplicative Markup)

Figure 9   The effect of doubling the interdiction rate along various
smuggling routes on value of cocaine imported

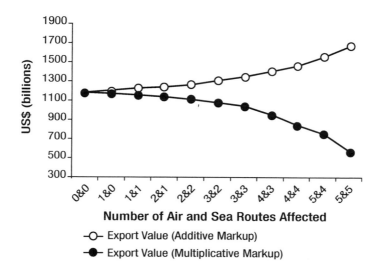

The above analysis applies specifically to the trafficking of cocaine from South to North America. But it also indicates some general limitations to interdiction programmes. As documented above, there are multiple cocaine and heroin trafficking routes into Europe from South America and Asia. The use of 'mules' – aeroplane passengers carrying small consignments – can be thought of as a 'backstop' smuggling method. It is not very efficient, but it is almost impossible to police. And it can be used to import drugs into any country in the world. As has been mentioned, the use of mules to carry heroin from Pakistan into Britain has increased markedly in the last few years – presumably in response to the more intensive policing of other routes. We can therefore assume that the pessimistic conclusions of the Caulkins, Crawford and Reuter model hold true of Britain as well as America.

(C) Low-level Enforcement

Data on drug retailing is even more unreliable and difficult to find than on production and trafficking. What is clear, however, that while manufacture and trafficking appear to be highly organised and to some degree oligopolistic, retailing is much more of a 'disorganised crime'. It is dominated by street gangs, their motorcycle counterparts and by independent sellers.

In the US, 'outlaw' motorcycle gangs such as the Pagans, Hells Angels and Bandidos are important wholesalers and retailers of methampetamines. Cocaine (especially in rock form) is sold by African-American Hispanic, Caucasian and Dominican street gangs, often associated with a larger 'umbrella' gang organisation such as the Mexican Mafia, the Latin Kings or Black Gangster Disciple Nation. These organisations will, like biker gangs, use the retailing of powder and rock cocaine as a source of revenue. The retailing of heroin is also dominated by street gangs and low-level independents. Well-organised wholesaling is the norm in Chicago and Los Angeles, but in other major drug centres there appear to be fewer middlemen and more direct contact between high-level wholesalers and retailers. At the retail level, 'local independent dealers, operating within specific communities or serving a specific clientele, are the norm... regardless of the source of the heroin'.[189]

Motorcycle gangs, increasingly armed with sophisticated weapons, are also important to the internal drug trade in Europe. But retailing in Western Europe is if anything even less organised than in the US. It is characterised by users who also deal, by licit businesses that sideline in drugs (such as nightclub doormen who sell Ecstasy and other club drugs), by networks of dealers who also consume drugs and know each other socially and by enterprising individuals.

The logic of drug retailing

Drug wholesalers face two conflicting incentives. There is strong incentive to move into lower level distribution, since there are large quantity discounts for illicit drugs and the bulk of accounting profits in the trade accrue to middle and lower level retailers rather than to high level 'Mr. Big' wholesalers. On the other hand, there is an incentive to focus on high-level distribution, as the probability of detection is greater for lower level wholesalers and retailers. This explains why, for instance, Colombian organisations are increasingly focussing on production and high-level distribution, while gradually off-loading mid- and low-level wholesaling onto their Dominican and Mexican associates.

Jonathan Caulkins constructs a model that formalises the trade off between these two incentives.[190] Dealers must decide where to position themselves in the supply tree. A position lower down the tree will increase their quantity discount. But it will also increase the number of customers they must supply and hence their risk of being caught by the police.

Using the Caulkins model, we can predict the effect of law enforcement initiatives that raise the costs of drug dealing. For a starting quantity discount, an increase in enforcement can have two effects. It can either push dealers further up the supply chain, or else it can induce them to lower their quantity discount. If enforcement succeeds in lowering quantity discounts, it will increase retail prices and, since demand is not inelastic, reduce consumption. The quantity discount factor for a number of illegal drugs is estimated to fall between 0.65 and 0.85. For a discount factor of 0.85, an enforcement effort that raised the costs of dealing by 10 per cent can be expected theoretically to increase retail prices by 10 per cent. For smaller factors, enforcement is more effective. For instance, when the discount is 0.75, a 10 per cent increase in costs can be expected to lower the discount factor to 0.7286 and boost prices by almost 16 per cent.

Conceivably, then, enforcement focused on dealers and distributors can be effective in reducing drug consumption. As the following table shows, enforcement efforts that boost the costs of drug dealing by 10 per cent can be expected to decrease heroin consumption by between 10 per cent and 29 per cent and decrease cocaine consumption by between 7 per cent and 32 per cent. The theoretical efficacy of such low-level enforcement depends crucially not only on the size of the discount factor, but also on one's estimate of demand elasticity for the relevant drugs. The following figures are derived from the various estimates of the demand elasticity of heroin and cocaine and from Caulkins's estimates of discount factors.

Table 8   The effect of low-level enforcement on the street price and consumption of heroin and cocaine

	Data Source	Elasticity	Price Change (10% cost increase, discount factor = 0.85)	Price Change (10% cost increase, discount factor = 0.75)	Change in Consumption (10% cost increase, discount factor = 0.85)	Change in Consumption (10% cost increase, discount factor = 0.75)
Heroin	Van Ours	-1.00	0.10	0.16	-0.10	-0.16
	Saffer and Chaloupka	-1.60	0.10	0.16	-0.16	-0.26
	Saffer and Chaloupka	-1.80	0.10	0.16	-0.18	-0.29

Table 8   *continued*

Cocaine	Saffer and Chaloupka	-0.66	0.10	0.16	-0.07	-0.11
	Saffer and Chaloupka	-1.10	0.10	0.16	-0.11	-0.18
	Grossman et al	-1.35	0.10	0.16	-0.14	-0.22
	Caulkins	-1.50	0.10	0.16	-0.15	-0.24
	Caulkins	-2.00	0.10	0.16	-0.20	-0.32

Low-level enforcement appears, then, to be an effective way of raising the retail price of illicit drugs. Caulkins and Reuter estimate that compensation received by dealers for risk of imprisonment accounts for some 23.6 per cent of cocaine retail prices. This is the second largest component of cocaine street prices after compensation to dealers for risk of physical harm (33 per cent).[191]

Unfortunately, the available data does not offer any support for these theoretical predictions. One would expect, on the basis of Caulkins's model, to find a negative correlation between arrests and consumption; the greater the number of arrests in connection with a particular drug, the lower one would expect the consumption of that drug to be. But both the number of arrests for cocaine and heroin offences *and* the consumption of the two drugs have fallen over the last 11 years in the US, as is demonstrated by the following graph.

Figure 10   Arrests for cocaine and heroin offences and total heroin and cocaine consumption in the US[192]

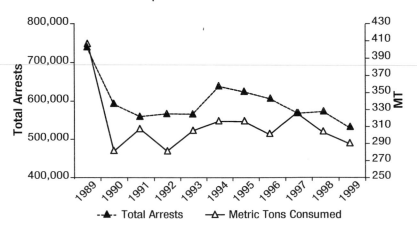

Mapping arrests against price one gets similarly uninspiring results. Cocaine and heroin arrests rose spectacularly during the 1980s (from 87,900 in 1982 to 735,300 in 1989) while the price of both drugs fell steadily. After 1990, arrests remained roughly constant; meanwhile cocaine and heroin prices continued their secular decline.

Figure 11   Arrests for cocaine and heroin offences and the street-price of cocaine in the US[193]

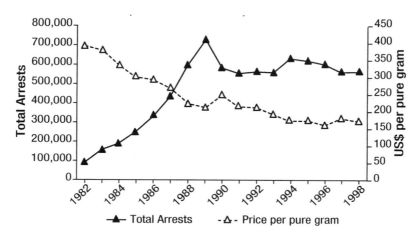

What is the meaning of these puzzling statistics? John DiNardo, in his study of material from the STRIDE database, concludes that enforcement has a statistically insignificant impact on price and use.[194] But enforcement and price do not in fact exist in the simple world implied by the words *ceteris paribus*. It is quite possible that enforcement has a positive effect upon price, but that this is masked by falling factory gate prices for drugs. Another conclusion might be that enforcement and use are endogenous. But it is also possible that lower dealer rents or large supplier inventories cushion drug prices. What is certain is that escalating low-level enforcement does not have the clearly positive effects on price that its proponents would hope for.

Conclusion: Some unpleasant lessons for supply-side policy
The first lesson is that programmes like crop substitution, while they may well be desirable in their impact on incomes in producer countries, are a poor way of increasing drug prices and decreasing drug use.

The second lesson is that crop or production destruction is an even bigger waste of resources. Unlike crop substitution, such programmes have no advantages for residents of producer countries. Like crop substitution, they have little effect on retail drug prices and thus are ineffective in lowering drug use.

The third lesson is that interdiction programmes are likely to be useful only if effort is concentrated on all possible routes of smuggling and mark-ups are fixed. If the additive price transmission mechanism is a better approximation of reality than the multiplicative, then these programmes are largely pointless. Whether the multiplicative or the additive model is better is not clear. One can argue that at the trafficking level, like the production level, rewards are proportional to quantity not price, and that the additive model should therefore be used, but this is not wholly compelling. It is therefore not clear whether interdiction is able to effect prices. However, the conclusion that interdiction must increase across *all* routes to have an appreciable impact on price may make it a very costly strategy.

The fourth lesson is perhaps the most painful of all. There are good theoretical reasons to suppose that lower-level enforcement activity can reduce the use of drugs, and indeed these theoretical arguments find some support in the large risk premium that dealers enjoy. However, these arguments are not clearly supported by the available data. This data shows no correlation at all between increases in enforcement activity and the price of drugs. Until more research has been done, it seems best to suspend judgement.

The conclusion of this essay is that supply-side measures designed to reduce the use of illegal drugs – and in particular heroin and cocaine – have not been proven to work. A vast amount of taxpayers' money is being spent with no evidence of a return. In particular, Keith Hellawell's confident assertion that government interventions 'have most impact.... further up the supply chain' is the precise reverse of the truth. What the current supply-side measures should be replaced with is another question entirely, and one that is beyond the scope of this essay.

9. HEROIN: THE CASE FOR PRESCRIPTION

INGO PIES AND CLAUDIA SCHOTT

The drug problem is not only a matter of health, but very often of life and death for the individual involved. Many people think that it is far too serious an issue to treat as a mere matter of economics. We are of exactly the opposite opinion: the drug problem is much too important to ignore the contribution that economics can make. Precisely *because* it is a matter of life and death, we need to consider whether the current policy of prohibition supplies the right incentives. After all, the black market in drugs is still a *market*. It is a market with certain peculiar features, which can be explained by economic theory. Economic analysis can both expose the contradictions of prohibition and help prepare the ground for a new conception of drug policy. Both are important to ensure that drug policy complies with the same standards of rationality established in most other areas of policy.

Aims of Heroin Policy

Debate about heroin policy is characterised by a collision between two sets of interest. On the one hand, there are the interests of heroin consumers. On the other, there are the interests of non-consumers. These two sets of interest can be spelt out as follows:

Table 1   Interests of consumers and non-consumers

Interests of Consumers	Interests of Non-consumers
Protection of consumer sovereignty	Protection of non-users against harm, including crime
Harm reduction	Prevention of the spread of heroin use

The interests of users include the protection of their consumer sovereignty and a set of goals generally referred to as 'harm reduction'. Both sets of interests would be best satisfied by a policy of decriminalisation. Many heroin users are casual or 'recreational'. Even among addicts, there are many that have a stable and manageable pattern of use. Such users object to the criminalisation of what they regard as a harmless and enjoyable private pursuit.[195] The decriminalisation of heroin would safeguard their privacy, their consumer sovereignty and, more generally, their human dignity. Chronic heroin users, who wish to end their habit, may be more interested in the provision of social and medical support than the legal status of heroin. They will be inclined to favour a policy of 'harm reduction', an umbrella name for all policies that seek to minimise the harm caused by drug addiction. But effective harm reduction policies are hard to implement without decriminalisation. Criminalisation prevents help reaching those who most require it. Programmes that demand abstinence do not appeal to all heroin users, and must therefore be supplemented with programmes that accept addiction and seek to manage its problems. But this in turn implies decriminalisation.

The main interest of non-consumers is to limit the social costs of heroin use and to prevent or discourage new users from taking up heroin. Non-users seek to protect first-time users – and especially first-time juvenile users – against the drug's dangerous addictive potential. This implies that heroin should be made more difficult or more expensive to obtain. In addition, non-users seek to prevent harm to third parties. In the first place, this implies the prevention of heroin-related crime. But measures against the spread of infectious diseases (such as hepatitis and AIDS) are implied as well.

Two assumptions underlie the policy of prohibition. The first is that there is a necessary trade-off between the interests of users and the interests of non-users. Policy must choose in favour either of one or the other. The second assumption is that the interests of non-users should be given priority over the interests of users. We can display these assumptions graphically. The first assumption underlying prohibition is that policy is situated at some point on a negatively sloping line. This line indicates a trade-off between the interests of users and non-users; improvements for one group are at the expense of the other. The second assumption is that policy should be located as far down the sloping line as possible. It should move from the current status quo q towards the point of maximum repression p. In other words, the interests of non-users take precedence over the interests of users. Line c represents the constitutional constraints that have to be considered. We would not, for example, countenance the execution of heroin users, even if this could be shown to achieve the goal of eliminating heroin use.

Figure 1   A Prohibitionist View of Heroin Policy

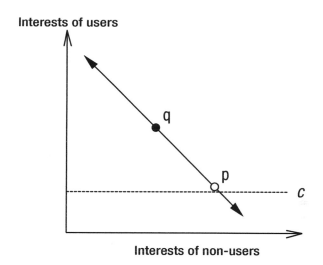

Interests of users

Interests of non-users

This essay questions the first and fundamental assumption underlying prohibition. It questions the existence of a trade-off between the interests of users and non-users. Is it really the case that a policy of prohibition is necessary to protect the vulnerable against the temptation of heroin use, and to protect third parties against the damage wrought by heroin? Might it not, in fact, undermine both these aims? Might not the interests of *both* users *and* non-users be better served by a less repressive policy?

The intentions and actual effects of heroin prohibition

A policy of prohibition is designed to suppress the market for drugs. It typically involves both supply-side and demand-side measures. Actions taken on the supply side are designed to force up the costs of production, and thus increase the prices illegal suppliers must charge in order to cover their expenses. Measures taken on the demand side are intended to reduce the quantity of drugs consumers are willing to purchase at any given price. Supply-side measures shift the supply curve (indicating the quantity of drugs that suppliers will supply at any given price) up and to the left. Demand-side measures shift the demand curve (indicating the quantity of drugs that consumers will consume at any given price) down and to the left. If demand-side measures are more effective than supply-side measures, then both the equilibrium price per unit of drug and the equilibrium quantity of drugs consumed will fall. If supply-side measures are more effective, then the equilibrium price will rise but the quantity of drugs consumed will fall. If they are of equal efficacy, then the price will stay the same and the amount of drugs consumed will fall.

Prohibition can result in two different scenarios. The first is a *shrinking* market. The quantity exchanged between suppliers and consumers declines. The effect on the price is unpredictable though. The price-reducing effect of declining demand is compensated – and may be even over-compensated – by the price-increasing effect of declining supply. Figure 2 shows a situation in which these two effects exactly cancel each other out, and the price remains the same after prohibition (the market equilibrium shifts from E to E*). A stronger effect on the supply side would result in higher prices, whereas a stronger effect on the demand side would result in lower prices.

Figure 2   The effect of prohibition: a diminished market

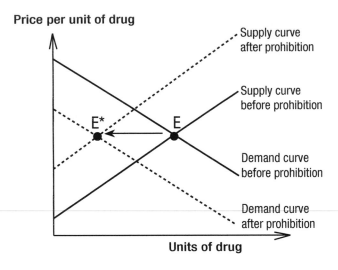

The second scenario is a complete *dissolution* of the market. Here, the impact of policy on consumers and suppliers is sufficient to destroy the market for drugs altogether. The supply and demand curves have moved so much that they no longer intersect. The exchange of goods comes to a halt, because the maximum price that the consumer is willing to pay (P_D) is now lower than the minimum price (P_S) that the supplier requires to cover his costs.

Figure 3   The effect of prohibition: a dissolved market

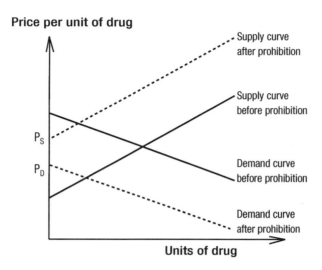

Price per unit of drug

P_S

P_D

Supply curve
after prohibition

Supply curve
before prohibition

Demand curve
before prohibition

Demand curve
after prohibition

Units of drug

Having described some of the economic theory, we turn now to the practice of prohibition. It is noteworthy that prohibition has not so far succeeded in dissolving the market for heroin. On the contrary, we now have an established black market which functions in such a way that none of the four aims of drug policy set out earlier has been achieved.

1   Protection of consumer sovereignty

Prohibition criminalises consumers who inflict no harm on any third party, and who regard their consumption as a legitimate private pastime. This is a major violation of their sovereignty, which is tolerated only on the assumption that it is necessary for the protection of non-consumers.

2   Harm reduction

The illegality of heroin massively increases the harm it inflicts on users. It does so in two different ways. Illegal heroin is several times more expensive than legal heroin. This is because its suppliers need to impose a risk surcharge to cover the cost of possible arrest and conviction, and because illegal markets are especially conducive to monopoly. Many addicts are unable to finance their habit by legitimate means, and so resort to theft, prostitution or drug dealing. They are forced into the criminal underworld.

The illegality of heroin also exacts a severe toll on users' health. In a legal market there are regulations designed to shield consumers from harm; in a black market there are none. Consumers of illegal heroin have no redress against fraud or adulteration. Almost all street heroin is 'cut' with other substances, many of them noxious. And the varying purity of street heroin exposes its users to a high risk of overdosing. As the table below shows, the vast majority of deaths among German heroin addicts are caused by overdosing. When heroin was made available on prescription in Switzerland, the number of deaths from overdosing dropped to zero (see figure 6). We can conclude that the majority of German heroin addicts are killed not by heroin but by the law against heroin.

Figure 4   Causes of death of German drug users[196]

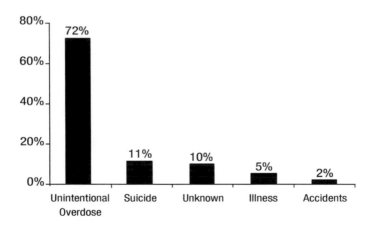

3   Protection of non-users against harm, including crime

A heroin addict commits a crime every time he or she purchases heroin. On top of this, the hugely inflated cost of illegal heroin forces many addicts to commit theft. According to a careful estimate, the total costs of heroin-related crime in Germany in 1992 ran at around 6 billion DM. That works out at approximately 78 DM (£25) per capita. Even excluding the distress caused to individual victims, that is a massive burden on society. Quite clearly, prohibition is failing in its aim of protecting non-users against harm.

Table 2   The costs of drug-related crime in Germany, 1992[197]

Drug trafficking related crime	DM millions	GBP millions
Cost for police	408.40	130.20
Judicial costs	146.50	46.70
Cost of imprisonment	589.40	187.90
Other drug-related crime (harm to third parties)		
Cost of offences	3,223.20	1,027.56
Cost for police	1,288.30	410.71
Judicial Costs	369.20	117.70
Cost of imprisonment	237.80	75.81
Total	6,262.80	1,996.58

4   Prevention of the spread of heroin use

Perhaps most surprising of all, it is not at all obvious that the current policy of prohibition is the best way of preventing the spread of heroin use. The misery it inflicts on addicts can be assumed to have some deterrent effect. But there are strong economic grounds for thinking that this is offset by other effects. The high price of illegal heroin, as has already been mentioned, forces many addicts to deal to support their habit. Consumers form the bulk of street-level suppliers. They do the risky final deal on the street, thereby functioning as a cushion of sorts between the drug gangs and the police.[198] This creates a highly decentralised network of dealers. Each dealer has a strong incentive to recruit more customers, to keep himself in pocket and possibly also to climb up the organisation's internal hierarchy. Each new customer, once hooked on the drug, becomes a potential dealer. In this way, the market for heroin expands geometrically. Far from protecting non-users against heroin, current policy ensures that it is made available to an ever-increasing number.

The illegal market for heroin has another perverse effect. Studies show that first-time consumers usually obtain their heroin in a social environment. Most of these first-time users are charged below-market prices; they pay nothing or next to nothing.[199] At first blush, such 'hand-outs' seem surprising, but there is an economic rationale behind them. They are based on two well-known economic laws, both of which can be observed in legal as well as illegal markets. First, these gifts are used to reduce informational asymmetry. By supplying free or inexpensive samples, the dealer tries to convince the new customer of the quality and purity of his product. He is doing exactly what legal companies do when they offer free samples, test packages or personal presentations. Secondly, these gifts are examples of the so-called 'subscription effect'. It is worthwhile to invest in a long-term customer relationship. Other examples of the subscription effect include the free gifts that shopkeepers sometimes give to valued customers. These marketing incentives undermine the protection for first-time users and juveniles that prohibition purports to provide.

At this point another aspect of prohibition should be emphasised. Both in public opinion and in the specialist literature, the rationality of addiction is a highly contested topic.[200] If, as some economists and psychologists suggest, drug addicts act irrationally because they systematically underestimate the long-term costs of present drug use, the price policy of heroin sellers in the black market is especially dangerous. If first-time users pay low prices and addicts higher prices, then the cost of underestimating future harms is even greater than it would be were prices constant. Prohibition tends to worsen the problems faced by people who underestimate future costs and overestimate present benefits. If – as is often claimed – it is young people who are most prone to this form of irrationality, then prohibition is especially damaging to them.

A preliminary conclusion is that prohibition both violates the rights of heroin users and maximises the dangers of heroin use. Moreover, this neglect of the interests of users is *not* counterbalanced by any success in satisfying of the interests of non-users. The prohibition of heroin instead creates incentives for users to commit drug-related crimes and to recruit new users. Prohibition is not part of the solution; it is part of the problem.

The Dilemma of Prohibition

Confronted with these insights, supporters of prohibition might argue that the failure of prohibition thus far is simply a result of insufficient effort or expenditure. They might argue that we are in need of *more* and *stronger* repressive measures in order to effect the complete dissolution of the heroin market. This is not, however, a sensible conclusion to draw. The experience of America shows that even a considerable intensification of enforcement will not dissolve the market for drugs. In Europe, such measures are outside the bounds of realistic policy. As has already been mentioned, there are constitutional constraints – both legal and moral – on the enforcement of prohibition. In Europe, these constraints are more severe than in America. Most of the relevant authorities consider drug addiction as a medical rather than a criminal problem. This tendency was given a good deal of encouragement by the emergence of AIDS in the mid-1980s, one consequence of which was the introduction of methadone programmes and needle exchanges throughout

Europe. A kind of grudging tolerance was thereby extended to opiate use.

This poses an insoluble dilemma for prohibition. To be really effective, prohibition must increase the costs of heroin use. But to the extent that policy delivers a wide range of support measures for users – summarised by the slogan 'therapy instead of punishment' – it tends to frustrate this goal. Prohibition can only succeed if it is inhumane; humane measures undermine prohibition. In this perverse situation, people involved with the drug problem – doctors, police officers, judges, public prosecutors and social workers – can only make things worse. Among such people there is an immense disillusionment with prohibition. This disillusionment goes some way towards explaining the fact that day-to-day practice no longer conforms to the letter of the law. Unwillingness to enforce prohibition is a partial explanation for the falling street price of heroin. Not a decline in demand, but less repression – enhanced by a Europe without borders – is the most likely explanation for this fall in price.[201]

An Economic Perspective on Reform

Our conclusion so far is that prohibition in its current form tends to frustrate all four sets of interest outlined above, and that it cannot be intensified any further. Figure 1 is thus a grossly misleading characterisation of the relationship between the interests of users and non-users. It is rather Figure 5, in which the interests of users and non-users are equated, that represents the real situation and the relevant alternatives for policy.

Figure 5   An economic perspective on reform

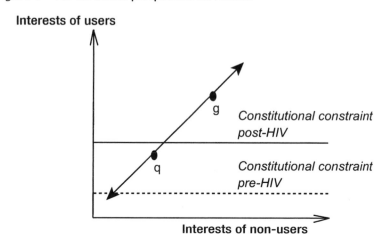

Interests of users

g   *Constitutional constraint post-HIV*

q   *Constitutional constraint pre-HIV*

Interests of non-users

Here we can see that the status quo (point q as before) is characterised by such a grave violation of consumers' interests that it does not comply even with the minimum constitutional standards of today. (Hence the widespread refusal to enforce the law.) Prohibition criminalises drug users and multiplies their health risks. It leads to wholly avoidable deaths. The status quo also produces perverse marketing incentives that do nothing to limit the spread of heroin to new users – most notably juveniles. Additionally, prohibition boosts heroin prices and therefore encourages criminality amongst addicts.

A rational drug policy must eschew prohibition. Prohibition fails to satisfy the interests of consumers and non-consumers alike. The assumed trade-off between the interests of users and non-users, which forms the basis of prohibitionist arguments, is a fiction. On the contrary, it is possible simultaneously to make *both* groups better off. Starting from point q in figure 10, it is possible to reach a point g that corresponds to higher utility for *both* users and non-users. Such a point is the realistic goal for a drug policy that accords equal weight to the interests of *all* citizens.

In order to achieve all four goals outlined above, a new institutional arrangement is needed. The current black market produces heavily distorted incentives. It lures in new customers with a subsidised product, while extracting high prices from the already addicted. This form of price discrimination should be reversed. Drug-related crime will only disappear when drug addicts are relieved of their financial pressures. At the same time, the entry of first-time users into the heroin market can only be discouraged with high as opposed to the currently subsidised prices. Furthermore, health risks can only be limited if there is a constant supply of non-adulterated heroin to existing addicts and regulated locations for its consumption. And finally, drug users can only live more or less normal lives when they are not criminalised for consumption.

There is a single solution to all four problems. Heroin should be made available on prescription to registered addicts. Its production should be opened up to regulated competition. Meanwhile, the penalties against the sale of heroin to non-addicts should remain in force. A system of prescription would protect the interests both of addicts and also the public at large.

Opening the contract for heroin sales to the medical service up to legal competition would have a drastic effect on its price. Heroin is simply a partially refined agricultural commodity. Its production is not a technical challenge, nor is it costly. Opening the market to legal suppliers would eliminate the two reasons for high prices. Neither a risk surcharge nor a cartel surcharge would be included in the price of heroin. Under a system of prescription, the cost of a heroin user's average daily dose would be reduced to less than 10 DM (approximately £3.20). This could be paid either by the state or by the user. Either way, it would eliminate the financial crime currently committed by addicts to support their habit.

Prescription would also have a dramatic effect on the quality of heroin. The usual audits and guarantees that currently apply to all legal pharmaceuticals would be applied to heroin as well. The principle of producers' liability would come into effect. The health risks of heroin consumption – which, as we have seen, are largely due to factors connected with its illegality – could thus be substantially reduced.

A system of prescription would help to protect non-users, and in particular juveniles, against exposure to heroin. Prohibition has singularly failed in this respect. The black market in heroin provides incentives to dealers to seek out new users and to ensnare them with low prices and free samples. Only when the dependency of addicts on dealers is ended can these perverse incentives be eliminated. Of course, a system of prescription to registered addicts would not eliminate the black market in heroin entirely, since there would still be many non-addicts eager to try heroin. But it would have two effects that would severely undermine the foundations of the illegal market. Most street-level heroin dealers, as has been mentioned, are also addicts. They deal to finance their addiction. Were cheap heroin made available to them on prescription, they would no longer have any pressing reason to deal. Secondly, a system of prescription would destroy dealers' financial incentive to invest in new customers. Such an investment only pays dividends if long-term client relations can be established. But if new customers are transferred to the state on becoming addicts the investment is 'lost'. The current system of marketing ploys, including subsidised hand-outs, would lose its rationale. We can thus predict, on *a priori* grounds, that prescription would greatly reduce the exposure of non-users to heroin.

We conclude that making heroin available to addicts on prescription would lower its price, improve its quality, and eliminate the perverse incentives associated with the black market. Drug related crime would be reduced, consumer protection would be strengthened and the effective protection of non-users and juveniles would become possible.

A legal market for heroin: the experience of Switzerland
The only fully monitored experiment in heroin prescription bears out these hypotheses. In Switzerland, between 1994 and 1996, 1,146 long-term heroin

addicts with a record of treatment failure were accepted onto a programme of opiate maintenance. Some were prescribed morphine, some methadone and some heroin, in both injectable and cigarette form. The experiment was closely monitored, and the results were later confirmed by the World Health Organisation.[202]

It was found that the 'recruitment of patients, retention rate (the duration of continuing participation) and compliance (adherence to the treatment instructions) were better with the prescription of injectable heroin than with that of injectable morphine and methadone'. Among those patients prescribed heroin, the first of the three goals outlined at the beginning of this essay were all achieved.

Protection of consumer sovereignty and harm reduction

The general condition of patients improved substantially. According to the WHO report, 'the number of homeless participants reduced from 12 per cent at entry to 1 per cent at 18 months.... The percentage of participants holding a job rose from 14 per cent to 32 per cent. The level of financial debt of study participants fell during the course of the study. While 15 per cent were debt-free at admission, at 18 months this had risen to 34 per cent.'[203] The average health of participants improved as well. Perhaps the most striking statistic is the complete eradication of fatal overdoses over the course of the experiment. (Compare this to the 71 per cent of deaths from overdose among German heroin addicts.) The largest single cause of death among participants in the Swiss project was AIDS. However, all but three AIDS infections were contracted *before* the beginning of the programme, and those three were 'very probably related to cocaine injected outside the programme'.[204]

Figure 6   Causes of death among Swiss patients[205]

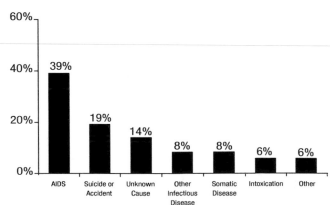

Protection of non-users against harm, including crime

The Swiss experiment also benefited non-users. According to the WHO report, 'police reports of criminal activity involving participants fell during the course of the study. In particular, the number of shop-lifting offences and the number of breaking and entry offences reported by participants or recorded by the police were reduced. The offences registered by the police reduced in excess of 50 per cent over the time of the study.[206] A cost-benefit analysis of the project revealed an average economic benefit of 95.5 Swiss franks per patient per day, the greatest part of which consisted in savings to the police and prison services, followed by savings to the health service. Given that the total costs of treatment equalled 51 Swiss franks per patient per day, the project more than paid for itself.[207]

Prevention of the spread of heroin use

Unfortunately, the write-up of the Swiss experiment did not investigate the effects of the project on the surrounding black market in heroin. It only reported that there had been no 'leakage' of legal heroin onto the black market; unsurprisingly, since patients were required to take their prescription on site. But evidence from the few clinics in Britain that until recently prescribed heroin suggest that it did indeed undermine the neighbouring black market. Sue Edwards, a social worker at the Clwyd Drug Service, reported that prior to the prescription of heroin there had been a organised black market in the region. 'She actively targeted dealers, particularly user/dealers, and was successful in getting them onto a prescription. She says that this removed their need to deal on a day-to-day basis because a) they now had the drug of their choice so they no longer needed to deal; b) the chance of losing the guaranteed daily dosage was too great a risk to take; and c) sheer economics told them that the market had disappeared.[208] This confirms exactly the prediction made earlier in the essay on the basis of pure economic theory.

Conclusion

Among the general public, there is a strong underestimation of the extent to which prohibition fails even according to its own standards. Consequently, it is important not to discuss the well-meaning *intentions* of prohibition but rather to focus on the *actual effects* of prohibition.

The actual effects of prohibition are to criminalise, impoverish and kill users, to force them to commit crimes against third parties and to create incentives for them to entice new users. Contrary to the claims of prohibitionists, the aims of users and non-users are not opposed. It is possible to construct a rational drugs policy that benefits both groups. We hope to have demonstrated that prescription is just such a policy.

CONTRIBUTORS

James Bakalar is Lecturer in Law in the Department of Psychiatry at Harvard Medical School and editor of the *Harvard Mental Health Letter*. He is the author or co-author of five books and numerous articles and chapters on mental health and public policy issues. Among his books are *Drug Control in a Free Society* (Cambridge University Press, 1984) and *Marihuana: The Forbidden Medicine* (Yale University Press, 1993), both co-authored with Lester Grinspoon.

Selina Chen is Head of Research at the Social Market Foundation.

Richard Davenport-Hines is a historian and biographer. His next book, *The Pursuit of Oblivion: A Narcotic History of the World, 1500-2000*, is due to be published by Weidenfeld and Nicolson in the autumn of 2001.

Diana V. Gardner is a doctoral student in political philosophy at Nuffield College, Oxford and a graduate of the University of Auckland. She is currently completing her thesis on the value of autonomy and the degree to which individuals should be allowed to contract away their future liberty.

Peter Lilley is Member of Parliament for Hitchin and Harpenden. He was appointed Secretary of State for Social Security 1992-1997, having joined Mrs. Thatcher's Cabinet as Secretary of State for Trade and Industry in 1990. Prior to that, he held the posts of Economic Secretary to the Treasury and Financial Secretary to the Treasury. He ran for the leadership of the Conservative Party in June 1997, subsequently becoming Shadow Chancellor and Deputy Leader of the Conservative Party responsible for overseeing renewal of policy until June 1999.

Donald McCarthy is currently Research Economist at the Milken Institute in Santa Monica, California. He was previously Economics Researcher at the Social Market Foundation's Centre for Post-Collectivist Studies and before that, a Research Officer at the Public Policy Group of the London School of Economics. He is author of *Annuities: The Case for Change*, published by the Social Market Foundation in May of 2000.

Ian McLaughlin is serving a life sentence in H.M.P. Lancaster.

Geoffrey Pearson is Wates Professor of Social Work at Goldsmiths College, University of London and editor of the *British Journal of Criminology*. He served as a member of the Independent Inquiry into the Misuse of Drugs Act, and is Vice-Chair of DrugScope, the UK's leading independent drugs information agency. His published work includes *The Deviant Imagination, Hooligan: A History of Respectable Fears, and The New Heroin Users*. His most recent research has included a study of middle-market drug distribution for the Home Office, and of patterns of drug use among young people in care for the Economic and Social Research Council.

Ingo Pies is Group Leader on Economic Policy at the Free University of Bozen-Bolzano and Deputy Chair of Economic and Social Policy at Passau University. He is co-editor of the publication series, *Konzepte der Gesellschaftstheorie*. He has written several books and articles on drugs and drug policy, including *Rationale Drogenpolitik in der Demokratie* (with Karl-Hans Hartwig), and 'Drogen' in *Handbuch der Wirtschaftsethik*.

Claudia Schott graduated in 1998 from Bochum University. Since October 1998 she has worked at the Department of Economics of Muenster University as a research assistant and assistant teacher. From October 2000 to June 2001 she worked for 'Policy Consult – Institute for Scientific Policy Solutions', where she participated in a project on giving out heroin to drug addicts under medical monitoring.

Edward Skidelsky is a doctoral student at Balliol College, Oxford, where he is writing a thesis on the philosophy of Ernst Cassirer. He writes regularly for the *New Statesman, The Telegraph, Prospect* and T*he Times Literary Supplement*.

Robert Skidelsky is Professor of Political Economy at Warwick University and was made a life peer in 1991. He is the author of several works including *Politicians and the Slump, John Maynard Keynes Vols. 1, 2 & 3* and *The World After Communism*.

Notes

Preface

1   *Drugs and the Law: Report of the Inquiry into the Misuse of Drugs Act*, London: The Police Foundation, 2000, paragraph 2.49, p.32. Cf. also the essay by Geoffrey Pearson in this volume.

2   Mark Tran, *The Guardian*, 31 Mar 2000.

Introduction

3   One the most influential statements of this pseudo-scientific theory was Gabriel Nahas, *Keep Off the Grass*, London: Pergamon, 1979. 'It appears that the biochemical changes induced by marijuana in the brain result in a drug-seeking, drug taking behaviour, which in many instances will lead the user to experiment with other pleasurable substances. The risk of progressing from marijuana to cocaine or heroin is now well documented.'

4   Cf. the essay by Richard Davenport Hines in this volume.

5   *Drugs and the Law: Report of the Inquiry into the Misuse of Drugs Act*, London: The Police Foundation, 2000, paragraph 2.64, p. 35.

6   Thomas Szasz, *Ceremonial Chemistry: The Ritual Persecution of Drugs, Addicts and Pushers*, New York: Anchor Press, 1974, p. xvii.

7   Quoted in Richard Davenport Hines, *The Pursuit of Oblivion*, published later in 2001 by Weidenfeld and Nicolson.

8   Jean Cocteau, *Opium: The Diary of a Cure*, London: Icon Books, 1957, p. 25. Cf. the famous opening sequence of the film *Trainspotting* for the expression of a very similar thought.

9   Anne Marlow, *How to Stop Time: Heroin from A to Z*, London: Virago, 1999, p. 144.

10 Geoffrey Pearson, *The New Heroin Users*, Oxford: Blackwell, 1987, p. 142.

11 J. S. Blackwell, 'Drifting, Controlling and Overcoming: Opiate Users who Avoid Becoming Chronically Dependent', *Journal of Drug Issues*, 13, no. 2, 1983, p. 228.

12 *Introductory Guide to the 1998 Crime and Disorder Act*, London: Home Office, 1998.

13 Cf. Sally A. Satel, 'Is Drug Addiction a Brain Disease' in Philip B. Heymann and William N. Brownsberger eds., *Drug Addiction and Drug Policy*, Cambridge Mass.: Harvard University Press, 2001, pp. 118-143.

14 Richard Stevenson, *Winning the War on Drugs*, London: IEA, 1994, p. 37.

15 *Ibid*, p. 57.

16 For an interesting discussion of the 'high-low' problem, cf. David T. Courtwright, *Forces of Habit*, Cambridge: Harvard University Press, 2001, pp. 152-166.

17 William A. McKim, *Drugs and Behaviour*, Englewood Cliffs: Prentice-Hall, 1986, p. 56.

18 *Drugs: The Need for Action*, Labour Party Document, 11 February 1994.

19 Ambros Uchtenhagen, Felix Gutzwiller and Anja Dobler-Mikola (eds.), *Programme for a Medical Prescription of Narcotics: Final Report of the Research Representatives*, Institut for Sozial-und-Praeventivmedizin der Universitaet Zuerich, 1997, p. 4.

20 Report of the External Panel on the Evaluation of the Swiss Scientific Studies of Medically Prescribed Narcotics to Drug Addicts, World Health Organisation, April 1999.

21 Jurgen Rehm, P. Gswend, T. Steffen et al, "Feasibility, safety and efficacy of injectable heroin prescription for refractory opioid addicts: a follow-up study" The Lancet, 358: 1417-20, 2001

22 Peter Edwards, *They Don't Become Angels*, A research project funded by the Australia-Britain Society, the Australian National Drug Crime Prevention Fund and the Tasmania Police, February, 1997.

23 J. A. Marks. 'Practice in a Provincial Drug Dependency Clinic.' Unpublished. November 1984, p. 3.

24   Mike Gray, 'Alert: Liverpool Clinic to Lose Funding on April 1', *Los Angeles Times*, February 1995.
25   *Ibid.*
26   Peter Edwards, *op. cit.*
27   Quoted in Peter Edwards, *op. cit.*
28   Cf. Uchtenhagen, Felix Gutzwiller and Anja Dobler-Mikola (eds.), *op. cit.*, p. 5, 'Those patients admitted to the project who had previously been following methadone substitution treatment had continued to use illicit heroin to a large extent during their methadone treatment.'
29   R. Newcombe, 'Methadone Mortality: Are British Drug Treatment Services Neglecting the Main Harmful Effects of Prescribing Methadone?' Discussion paper for the conference, *Drug Policy in the 90s: The Changing Climate*, Liverpool: 3D Research Bureau, June 1995, p. 2. Cf. also John Marks, 'Deaths from methadone and heroin', *The Lancet*, vol. 343, 16 April, 1994.
30   Peter Edwards, *op. cit.*
31   John Marks, *Drug Laws: A Case of Collective Psychosis*, London: The Libertarian Alliance, 1993, p.1.
32   Ambros Uchtenhagen, Felix Gutzwiller and Anja Dobler-Mikola (eds.), *op. cit.*, p. 8.
33   J. A. Marks, *State-Rationed Drugs: an Absurd Policy?* Unpublished, September 1987, p. 7.
34   Cf. H. Parker and P. Kirby, *Methadone Maintenance and Crime Reduction on Merseyside*, Crime Detection and Prevention Series, Paper 72, Police Research Group: London, 1996, p. 27.
35   Cf. Roy Egginton and Howard Parker, *op. cit.*

The History of British Drug Law
36   William B. McAllister, *Drug Diplomacy in the Twentieth Century*, London: Routledge, 1999, p. 218.
37   Joseph F. Spillane, *Cocaine: From Medical Marvel to Modern Menace in the United States 1884-1920*, Washington: John Hopkins University Press, 2000, p. 157.
38   Cf. Richard Davenport-Hines, *The Pursuit of Oblivion: a global history of narcotics 1500-2000*, London: Weidenfeld and Nicolson, 2001, pp. 154-8.
39   Cf. David T. Courtwright, *Dark Paradise: opiate addiction in America before 1940*, 1982, pp. 83-6, 95-6, 101-3, 108-12; Richard Davenport-Hines, *op. cit.*, pp. 165-6.
40   Sir William Collins, 'The Work of the International Opium Conference at The Hague', *Contemporary Review*, vol. 101, 1912, pp. 321-4.
41   Cf. David T. Courtwright, *op. cit.*, pp. 106-7, and Richard Davenport-Hines, *op. cit.*, pp. 177-80.
42   Public Record Office, Home Office, 45/11013/323566, Malcolm Delevingne, minute of 24 February 1917.
43   Sir Malcolm Delevingne, 'The International Background to the Dangerous Drugs Acts', in Sir Hugh Linstead, *Poisons Law*, 1936, p. 134.
44   Public Record Office, Home Office, 144/6073/436328/32, minute of M. D. Perrins, 20 February 1924.
45   Public Record Office, Home Office, 144/6073/436328/58, memorandum of Dr. A. Mahfooz Bey, 5 December 1924.
46   Westel W. Willoughby, *Opium as an International Problem*, 1925, p. 379.
47   Elystan Morgan, *House of Commons Debates*, 25 March 1970, vol. 798, col. 1555.
48   Lord Haldane, *House of Lords Debates*, 28 July 1925, vol. 125, cols. 457-9.
49   For further details cf. Richard Davenport-Hines, *op. cit.*, pp. 188-9.
50   A. J. Douthwaite, 'The Ban on Heroin', *British Medical Journal*, 9 April 1955, pp. 907-8, was the first of a stream of letters from physicians protesting against the proposed ban on the medical use of heroin. Cf. Richard Davenport-Hines, *op. cit.*, pp. 304-5.
51   Cf. Philip Bean ed., *Cocaine and Crack: Supply and Use*, New York: Houndmills, 1993, especially Bean's essay 'Cocaine and Crack: the Promotion of an Epidemic', pp. 59-75.

52 For a first-class account of Rohypnol, see Philip Jenkins, *Synthetic Panics: the Symbolic Politics of Designer Drugs*, New York: New York University Press, 1999, pp. 160-182.

53 Cf. Stanley Cohen, *Folk Devils and Moral Panics*, London: MacGibbon and Kee, 1972, p. 56 and Paul Barker, 'Brighton Battleground', *New Society*, 21 May 1964, p. 10.

54 See the Rev. Kenneth Leech, *A Practical Guide to the Drug Scene*, London: S.P.C.K., 1972 and *Keep the Faith, Baby*, London: S.P.C.K., 1973 for authoritative references to early patterns of British LSD use by the secretary of the Soho Drugs Group.

55 James Callaghan, *House of Commons Debates*, 27 January 1969, vol. 776, col. 959.

56 Richard Crossman, *The Diaries of a Cabinet Minister*, vol. III, London: Hamish Hamilton, 1977, p. 808.

57 *Ibid*, p. 837.

Soft Drugs and Paternalism

58 *Tackling Drugs to Build a Better Britain: United Kingdom Anti-Drugs Coordinator's First Annual Report and National Plan*, London: Cabinet Office, 1999, p. 3.

59 *Drugs and the Law: Report of the Inquiry into the Misuse of Drugs Act*, London: The Police Foundation, 2000, p. 1.

60 Richard Stevenson, *Winning the War on Drugs*, London: IEA, 1994, p. 13-14.

61 Ralph Weisheit, 'Declaring a 'Civil' War on Drugs', in *Drugs, Crime and the Criminal Justice System*, ed. Ralph Weisheit, Cincinnati: Anderson Publishing Co., 1990, pp.1-5. Quoted in Donald Husak, *Drugs and Rights*, Cambridge: Cambridge University Press, 1992, p. 125.

62 U.S. Department of Labor, *What Works: Workplaces without Drugs*, Washington: U.S. Government Printing Office, 1991, p. 5. Quoted in Husak, *op. cit.*, p. 128.

63 Cf. *Drugs and the Law*, London: The Police Foundation, 2000, Chapter 3, paragraphs 16 and 30. See also the article by James Bakalar in this volume.

64 The philosophical problems surrounding addiction are vast and complex. I touch on them here not because I am deeply committed to any one position over another, but simply because I want to exclude the whole subject from consideration. Addiction raises a set of questions quite different from those raised by soft drugs. And any discussion of the legalisation of heroin and cocaine is at the present moment academic. For a further discussion of addiction, see the essays by James Bakalar and Diana Gardner in this volume.

65 Herder, *Ideen*, vii.I, in *Sämtliche Werke*, XIII, 291. Quoted in Charles Taylor, *Sources of the Self*, Cambridge: Cambridge University Press, 1989, p. 375.

66 Wilhelm von Humboldt, *The Limits of State Action*, Cambridge: Cambridge University Press, 1969, p. 28.

67 *Ibid*, p. 22.

68 John Stuart Mill, *On Liberty and Other Writings*, Cambridge: Cambridge University Press, 1989, p. 60.

69 *Ibid*, p. 62

70 *Tackling Drugs to Build a Better Britain*, London: The Stationery Office, 1998, p. 3.

71 Cf. essay by Peter Lilley in this volume for an assessment of the factual claims in this statement. Many of the government's statements on the dangers of soft drugs are false. But even if they were all true, my argument would not be affected.

72 Richard Stevenson, *op. cit.*, p. 13.

73 John Kaplan, *Marijuana: The New Prohibition*, New York: World Publishing Company, 1970, p. xi.

74 William Bennett, 'The Plea to Legalize Drugs is a Siren Call to Surrender' in *Drugs and Society*, ed. Michael Lyman and Garry Potter, Cincinnati: Anderson Publishing Co., 1991, p. 339.

75 James B. Bakalar and Lester Grinspoon, *Drug Control in a Free Society*, Cambridge: Cambridge

University Press 1984, p. 22.

76   William Bennett, *National Drug Control Strategy*, Washington: U.S. Government Printing Office, 1989, p. 11.

Addiction and Free Will

77   Robert E. Goodin, *No Smoking: The Ethical Issues*, Chicago: The University of Chicago Press, 1989, p. 98. He also writes, 'If it is autonomy that we are trying to protect in opposing paternalistic legislation in general, then the same values that lead us to oppose such legislation in general will lead us to welcome it in those particular cases where what we are being protected from is something that would deprive us of the capacity for autonomous choice.' *Ibid*, p. 27.

78   For a fuller discussion, see Harry G. Frankfurt's seminal article, 'Freedom of the Will and the Concept of a Person', *The Journal of Philosophy*, v. 68, n.1, January 1971.

79   Higher-order volitions do not have to be universalisable laws. A person might, for example, have a higher-order preference to stop smoking marijuana because her employer performs random drug tests and she wants to keep her job. It is perfectly consistent to want to give up cannabis oneself while not thinking that everyone else ought to give it up.

80   For more on the distinction between general self-directedness and perfect autonomy, see: Gerald Dworkin, *The Theory and Practice of Autonomy*, Cambridge: Cambridge University Press, 1988, ch.1; Stanley I. Benn, *A Theory of Freedom*, Cambridge: Cambridge University Press, 1988, ch.8; Robert Young, 'Autonomy and the 'Inner Self', in John Christman ed., *The Inner Citadel: Essays on Individual Autonomy*, New York: Oxford University Press, 1989; Lawrence Haworth, 'Dworkin on Autonomy', *Ethics*, v. 102, n.1, October 1991.

81   James B. Bakalar and Lester Grinspoon, *Drug Control in a Free Society*, Cambridge: Cambridge University Press, 1984, p.36.

82   Additionally, some cultures do not even have a concept of addiction. The fact of addiction may exist in those societies (that is, the pattern of drug use accords with what would be called addiction in England, for example) but members of the culture simply do not conceptualise it as such. See Jon Elster, *Strong Feelings: Emotion, Addiction, and Human Behavior*, Massachusetts: The MIT Press, 1999, pp. 114-5.

83   Philip Bean, 'Cocaine and Crack: The Promotion of an Epidemic', in *Cocaine and Crack: Supply and Use*, Philip Bean ed., Hampshire: The MacMillan Press Ltd, 1993, p. 70.

84   Jim Orford, *Excessive Appetites: A Psychological View of Addictions*, Chichester: John Wiley & Sons, 1985, pp. 194-5.

85   Kevin Williamson, *Drugs and the Party Line*, Edinburgh: Rebel Inc., 1997, pp. 109-110. Cf. the essay by Ingo Pies and Claudia Schott in this volume.

86   Jon Elster, *op. cit.*, p. 125.

87   Jim Orford, *Excessive Appetites: A Psychological View of Addictions*, Chichester: John Wiley & Sons, 1985, p.290.

88   Elster argues, for instance, that 'once a behavioral pattern is conceptualized as an addiction, with the concomitant causal beliefs, it may change dramatically' and 'to some extent, it doesn't matter whether a substance or behavioral pattern is actually addictive, as long as people believe it is.' See Jon Elster, *op. cit.*, p.129 and p.134. This suggests that it may be harmful (with regard to the person who is already addicted) to depict addiction as something impossible to overcome.

89   George Loewenstein, 'A Visceral Account of Addiction', in Jon Elster and Ole-Jorgen Skog eds., *Getting Hooked: Rationality and Addiction*, Cambridge: Cambridge University Press, 1999, p. 244.

90   *Ibid*, p. 245.

91 Dopamine neurones belong to the same family as adrenaline, noradrenaline and seratonin, all of which use biogenic amines as neurotransmitters. See O. T. Phillipson, 'Dopamine' in Richard L. Gregory ed., *The Oxford Companion to the Mind*, Oxford: Oxford University Press, 1987, p. 199.

92 Karen Young Kreeger, 'Drug Institute Tackles Neurology of Addiction', *The Scientist*, v. 9, n. 16, 21 August 1995, p. 13.

93 Avram Goldstein and Harold Kalant, 'Drug Policy: Striking the Right Balance', in Ronald Bayer and Gerald M. Oppenheimer eds., *Confronting Drug Policy: Illicit Drugs in a Free Society*, Cambridge: Cambridge University Press, 1993, p. 85, f. 8.

94 Eliot L. Gardner and James David, 'The Neurobiology of Chemical Addiction', in Jon Elster and Ole-Jorgen Skog, *op. cit.*

95 *Ibid*, p. 119.

96 Gardner and David assert that the cues are neurobiologically encoded in the brain.

97 Eliot L. Gardner and James David, *op. cit.*, p. 120.

98 See, for example, *Living Sober: Some methods A.A. members have used for not drinking*, York: A.A. General Service Office, 1975. Referring to another twelve-step program based on AA, Gardner and David describe a compulsive gambler playing the slot-machines in a manner visually and motivationally reminiscent of laboratory rats repeatedly self-administering drugs by pulling on a lever. They write, 'But this same gambler, the following year, choosing to attend a Gamblers Anonymous meeting rather than buy an airplane ticket to Las Vegas, looks a good deal less like our laboratory animals.' See Eliot L. Gardner and James David, *op. cit.*, p.127.

99 Interestingly, in Narcotics Anonymous it is suggested that recovering addicts also refrain from alcohol and mind-altering substances other than the ones they were addicted to.

100 If cross-priming does occur, this has implications for former addicts who require pain relief, for example, following an accident or surgery or during serious illness. Where drug use cannot reasonably be avoided, the former addict should (if possible) take precautions against subsequent craving responses.

101 See Harry G. Frankfurt, 'Identification and Wholeheartedness', *The Importance of What We Care About: Philosophical Essays*, Cambridge: Cambridge University Press, 1988.

102 Addicts usually claim that they have no desire to go on being addicted, but their testimony is not necessarily trustworthy. The widespread disapproval of drug use makes them understandably reluctant to admit to any desire to continue in their current way of life.

103 Jim Orford suggests that addiction cannot be overcome without such higher-order decision-making on the part of the addict. Cf. *Excessive Appetites: A Psychological View of Addictions*, Chichester: John Wiley & Sons, 1985, ch. 13 (esp. pp. 271-284).

104 *The Crime and Disorder Act 1998* (see sections 61-64) requires the drug user to consent to participation in the program, although treatment and testing are mandatory once agreed to. One of the Police Foundation's recommendations is that 'a drug treatment and testing order may not be appropriate for offenders who have been convicted of possession only.' See *Drugs and the Law: Report of the Independent Inquiry into the Misuse of Drugs Act*, London: The Police Foundation, chapter 5, paragraph 17.

105 Cf. Thomas Szasz, *Ceremonial Chemistry: The Ritual Persecution of Drugs, Addicts and Pushers*, New York: Anchor Press, 1974, p. xvii

The Varieties of Addiction

106 Cf. the essay by Diana Gardner in this volume. 1 American Psychiatric Association, Diagnostic and Statistical Manual of Mental Disorders, Fourth Edition, Text Revision, Washington D.C.: American Psychiatric Press, 2000.

107 American Psychiatric Association, *Diagnostic and Statistical Manual of Mental Disorders, Fourth*

Edition, Text Revision, Washington D.C.: American Psychiatric Press, 2000.

108   The reward system works by releasing the chemical neurotransmitter dopamine in the medial forebrain bundle. Injury or drugs that lower dopamine activity make the reward circuit less sensitive; addictive drugs suddenly intensify the activity of the transmitter, and their power is greatest what they infiltrate the brain rapidly by smoking or injection. The target is reached by various routes. Cocaine interferes with the process by which dopamine is reabsorbed into the cells that release it. Nicotine acts at a receptor for the neurotransmitter acetylcholine in the reward system and may prevent the enzyme monoamine oxidase from breaking up the dopamine molecule. Other drugs act indirectly on neurons that feed impulses into the dopamine system. Opiates, for example, work mainly at receptors for the brain's own morphine-like substances, the endorphins and enkephalins. These may constitute an alternative reward system, and there may be secondary systems employing serotonin and other neurotransmitters.

109   G. F. Koob and E. J. Nestler, 'The neurobiology of drug addiction', *Journal of Neuropsychiatry*, Clinical Neuroscience 9, 1997, pp. 482-87.

110   L.N. Robins, J.E. Helzer and D.H. Davis, 'Narcotic use in southeast Asia and afterward: An interim study of 898 Vietnam returnees', Archives of General Psychiatry, vol. 329, 1975, pp. 55-61.

111   In one experiment, rats were given a choice between plain water and water containing morphine, in a solution either sweetened with sugar or made bitter with quinine. The rats generally drank large amounts of the drug solution in the first few days and then settled at a moderate level that was lower if it contained quinine and higher if it contained sugar. After a few months, the experimenters took the drug out, left it out for several months, and put it back. Now some of the rats took much more than before, and their intake was no longer affected by quinine or sugar. Other objects of desire and aversion had lost their influence. This change occurred only when the rats were originally offered the alternative of plain water. If they were forced to drink the morphine solution, they responded like most medical morphine users, with a physical withdrawal reaction but no persistent urge to take the drug. They were not addicted because they had not chosen to use the drug and their motivation system was intact. Cf. J. Wolffgramm and A. Heyne, 'From controlled drug intake to loss of control: the irreversible development of drug addiction in the rat', *Behavioural Brain Research*, vol. 70, 1995, pp. 77-94.

112   D. S. Ramsay and S. C. Woods, 'Biological consequences of drug administration', *Psychological Review*, vol. 104, 1997, pp. 170-93.

113   M. A. Schuckit, 'Genetics of the risk for alcoholism', *American Journal of Addiction*, vol. 9, 2000, p. 103-12.

114   R. N. Nesse and K. C. Berridge, 'Psychoactive drug use in evolutionary perspective', *Science*, vol. 278, 1997, pp. 63-66.

115   G. F. Koob and S. B. Caine, 'Cocaine addiction therapy – are we partially there?' *Nature Medicine*, vol. 5, 1999, pp. 993-95.

116   W. R. Miller and S. Rollnick, *Motivational Interviewing: Preparing People to Change Addictive Behaviour*, New York: Guilford, 1991.

117   Project Match Research Group, 'Matching alcoholism treatments to client heterogeneity: Project Match post-treatment drinking outcomes', *Journal of Studies on Alcohol*, vol. 58, 1997, pp. 7-29.

118   A. M. Ludwig, 'Cognitive processes associated with "spontaneous" recovery from alcoholism', *Journal of Studies on Alcohol*, vol. 46, 1985, pp. 53-58.

119   L.N. Robins, 'Vietnam veterans' rapid recovery from heroin addiction: a fluke or a normal expectation?' *Addiction*, vol. 88, 1993, pp. 1041-54.

Drugs and Poverty

120 I. Chein, D. Gerard, R. Lee, and E. Rosenfeld, *The Road to H: Narcotics, Delinquency and Social Policy*, London: Tavistock, 1964.

121 Hughes, P.H., Barker, N.W., Crawford, G.A. , and Jaffe, J.H., 'The Natural History of a Heroin Epidemic', *American Journal of Public Health*, vol. 62, no. 7, 1972, pp. 995-1001.

122 P. H. Hughes, *Behind the Wall of Respect: Community Experiments in Heroin Addiction Control*, Chicago: University of Chicago Press, 1977, p. 75.

123 Cf. Hughes, P.H. and Crawford, G.A., 'A Contagious Disease Model for Researching and Intervening in Heroin Epidemics', *Archives of General Psychiatry*, vol. 27, 1972, pp. 189-205.

124 Cf. T. Williams, *The Cocaine Kids*, New York: Addison-Wesley, 1989; P. Bourgois, *In Search of Respect: Selling Crack in El Barrio*, Cambridge: Cambridge University Press, 1995; L. Maher, *Sexed Work: Gender, Race and Resistance in a Brooklyn Drug Market*, Oxford: Oxford University Press, 1997; S. Murphy and M. Rosenbaum, *Pregnant Women on Drugs: Combating Stereotypes and Stigma*, New Jersey: Rutgers University Press, 1999; and B. A. Jacobs, *Dealing Crack: The Social World of Street-corner Selling*, Boston: Northeastern University Press, 1999.

125 Cf. C. Reinerman and H.G. Levine eds., *Crack in America: Demon Drugs and Social Justice*, Berkeley: University of California Press, 1997, and J. Austin, M. A. Bruce, L. Carroll, P. L. McCall, and S. C. Richards, *The Use of Incarceration in the United States: National Policy White Paper*, National Policy Committee, American Society of Criminology, 2000

126 S. Haw, *Drug Problems in Greater Glasgow*, London: SCODA, 1985, p. 53.

127 Cf. G. Pearson, M. Gilman and S. McIver, *Young People and Heroin: An Examination of Heroin Use in the North of England*, London: Health Education Council, 1985, G. Pearson, *The New Heroin Users*, Oxford: Blackwell, 1987, and H. Parker, K. Baxk, and R. Newcombe, *Living With Heroin: The Impact of a Drugs 'Epidemic' on an English Community*, Milton Keynes: Open University Press, 1988.

128 Cf. T. Bennett, *Drugs and Crime: The Results of Research on Drug Testing and Interviewing Arrestees*, Home Office Research Study 183, London: Home Office, 1998, and T. Bennett, *Drugs and Crime: The Results of the Second Developmental Stage of the NEW-ADAM Programme*, Home Office Research Study 205, London: Home Office, 2000.

129 Cf. H. Parker, C. Bury and R. Egginton, *New Heroin Outbreaks Among Young People in England and Wales*, Crime Detection and Prevention Series, Paper 92, London: Home Office, 1998.

130 G. Pearson and K. Patel, 'Drugs, Deprivation and Ethnicity: Outreach Among Asian Drug Users in a Northern English City', *Journal of Drug Issues*, vol. 28, no. 1, 1998, pp. 199-224.

131 Cf. Stanton Peele & Richard J. DeGrandpre, 'Cocaine and the Concept of Addiction', *Addiction Research*, vol. 6, 1998, p. 235-263. Cf. also the essay by James Bakalar in this volume.

132 Cf. A. Power, *Estates on the Edge: The Social Consequences of Mass Housing in Northern Europe*, London: Macmillan, 1997.

133 N.E. Zinberg, *Drug, Set, and Setting: The Basis of Controlled Intoxicant Use*, New Haven: Yale University Press, 1984.

134 Cf. E. Preble and J. J. Casey, 'Taking Care of Business: The Heroin User's Life on the Street', *International Journal of Addiction*, vol. 4, 1969, pp. 1-24.

135 Howard Parker, Judith Aldridge and Roy Egginton eds., *UK Drugs Unlimited: New Research and Policy Lessons on Illicit Drug Use*, Houndsmill: Palgrave, 2001, p. 114.

136 *Report of the External Panel on the Evaluation of the Swiss Scientific Studies of Medically Prescribed Narcotics to Drug Addicts*, World Health Organisation, April 1999, Paragraph 5.1. See also the essay by Ingo Pies and Claudia Schott in this volume.

137 Advisory Council on the Misuse of Drugs, *Drug Misuse and the Environment*, London: HMSO, 1998, pp. 113-115.

138 *Tackling Drugs to Build a Better Britain: United Kingdom Anti-Drugs Coordinator's First Annual Report and National Plan*, London: Cabinet Office, 1999, p. 3.

139 *Spending Review 2000: New Public Spending Plans 2001-2004*, HM Treasury, Section V, Chapter 29.

140 *Tackling Drugs to Build a Better Britain: The Second National Plan*, London: The Cabinet Office, 2000, p. 17

141 C. P. Rydell and S. S. Everingham, *Controlling Cocaine: Supply Versus Demand Programs*, Santa Monica: RAND, 1994.

142 P. J. Turnbull, T. McSweeney, R. Webster, M. Edmunds and M. Hough, *Drug Treatment and Testing Orders: Final Evaluation Report*, Home Office Research Study 212, London: Home Office, 2000.

143 M.A. Kleinman, *Against Excess: Drug Policy for Results*, New York: Basic Books, 1992.

144 Cf. M. Ramsay and S. Partridge, *op. cit.*

145 Cf. G. Pearson, 'Normal Drug Use: Ethnographic Fieldwork Among an Adult Network of Recreational Drug Users in Inner London', *Substance Use and Misuse*, vol. 36, nos. 1 & 2, 2001, pp. 167-200.

146 'Dangerous Habits', *The Lancet*, vol. 352, no. 9140, November 14, 1998, p. 1565.

147 *Tackling Drugs to Build a Better Britain: United Kingdom Anti-Drugs Coordinator's First Annual Report and National Plan*, London: Cabinet Office, 1999, p. 3.

148 B. A. Jacobs, *Dealing Crack: The Social World of Street-corner Selling*, Boston: Northeastern University Press, 1999, p. 130.

Common Sense on Cannabis

149 *The Lancet*, vol. 352, November 14, 1998.

150 Source: European Monitoring Centre for Drugs and Drug Addiction (EMCDDA), 2000.

151 *Drug Policy in the Netherlands*, Netherlands Ministry of Health, 1995.

152 *Source: European Monitoring Centre for Drugs and Drug Addiction (EMCDDA), 2000.*

153 Sources: United States: *National Household Survey 1997 SAMHSA*, Office of Applied Studies, Washington DC; Netherlands: M. Abraham, P. Cohen, M. de Winter, *Licit and Illicit Drug Use in the Netherlands*, University of Amsterdam/Statistics, Netherlands, CEDRO.

154 Sources: Trimbos Institute Fact Sheet 9; from reply by John Denham to PQ by author, Hansard 25 June 2001 (expenditure on Reducing Availability plus Criminal Justice System); US Office of National Drug Control Policy, 'Drug Data Policy', April 1999.

155 Cf. Gary Becker and Kevin Murphy, 'A Theory of Rational Addiction', *Journal of Political Economy* 96, 1988, pp. 675-700.

Supply Reduction: Why it Doesn't Work

156 Economists do not believe that individuals *really* maximize a utility function. They do believe, however, that individuals can be sensibly thought of as acting 'as if' they were maximizing such a function. The distinction is important for economists, since they get tired of being told how foolish they are to believe that the man in the street has the mathematical acumen of a modern day Pascal.

157 Cf. Ted O'Donoghue and Matthew Rabin, *Addiction and Present-Biased Preferences*, unpublished paper, October 2000.

158 Jan van Ours, 'The price elasticity of hard drugs: the case of opium in the Dutch East Indies, 1923-1938', *Journal of Political Economy* 103 (2), 1995, pp. 261-79.

159 Howard Saffer and Frank J. Chaloupka, *The Demand for Illicit Drugs*, NBER Working Paper no. 5238, Cambridge Mass.: National Bureau of Economic Research, 1995.

160 Jonathan P. Caulkins, *Developing Price Series for Cocaine*, Santa Monica, California: RAND

Corporation, 1994.

161 Cf. Peter Reuter, *The Mismeasurement of Illegal Drug Markets*, Santa Monica, California: RAND Corporation, 1997.

162 *International Narcotics Control Strategy Report 1998*, Bureau for International Narcotics and Law Enforcement Affairs, 1998.

163 *Global Illicit Drug Tends 2000*, United Nations Office for Drug Control and Crime Prevention, 2000.

164 *International Narcotics Control Strategy Report 1998*, Bureau for International Narcotics and Law Enforcement Affairs, 1998.

165 Jonathan P. Caulkins and Peter Reuter, *What Price Data Tell Us About Drug Markets*, Pittsburgh, Pennsylvania: Working Paper, H. John Heinz III School of Public Policy and Management, Carnegie-Mellon University, 1998.

166 David Kennedy, Peter Reuter and Kevin Jack Riley, *A Simple Economic Model of Cocaine Production*, Santa Monica, California: RAND Corporation, 1993.

167 *Ibid.*

168 Specifically a Cobb-Douglas production function.

169 Internal prices are the sums of labour, intermediate GDP products and intermediate cocaine products.

170 David Kennedy, Peter Reuter and Kevin Jack Riley, *op. cit.*

171 Source: David Kennedy, Peter Reuter and Kevin Jack Riley, *op. cit.*

172 Source: David Kennedy, Peter Reuter and Kevin Jack Riley, *op. cit.*

173 Cf. Jonathan P. Caulkins and Peter Reuter, *op. cit.*

174 Source: David Kennedy, Peter Reuter and Kevin Jack Riley, *op. cit.*

175 Source: David Kennedy, Peter Reuter and Kevin Jack Riley, *op. cit.*

176 Jonathan Caulkins, *Modelling the Domestic Distribution Network for Illicit Drugs*, Santa Monica, California: RAND, 1998.

177 There is an important Trans-Atlantic Ecstasy trade involving Israeli traffickers and Dutch producers.

178 DEA Congressional Testimony, 15/1/2000

179 *International Narcotics Control Strategy Report 1998*, Bureau for International Narcotics and Law Enforcement Affairs, 1998.

180 *Global Illicit Drug Tends 2000*, United Nations Office for Drug Control and Crime Prevention, 2000.

181 Cf. *What America's Users Spend on Illegal Drugs, 1988-1998*, Office of National Drug Control Policy 2000.

182 Keith Hellawell, *UK Anti-drug Coordinator Annual Report, 1999-2000*, London: Cabinet Office, p. 1

183 *Spending Review 2000: New Public Spending Plans 2001-2004*, HM Treasury, Section V, Chapter 29.

184 Source: John Martin Corkery, *Drug seizure and offender statistics, United Kingdom, 1999*, London: Home Office, 2001.

185 Source: John Martin Corkery, *Drug seizure and offender statistics, United Kingdom, 1999*, London: Home Office, 2001.

186 Source: *What America's Users Spend on Illegal Drugs, 1988-1998*, Office of National Drug Control Policy 2000.

187 Jonathan P. Caulkins, Gordon Crawford and Peter Reuter, 'Simulation of Adaptive Response: A Model of Drug Interdiction', *Mathematical and Computer Modelling 17*, no. 2, 1992, pp. 37-52.

188 Source: Jonathan P. Caulkins, Gordon Crawford and Peter Reuter, *op. cit.*

189 *National Drug Threat Assessment 2000 – The Domestic Perspective*, National Drug Intelligence Center.
190 Jonathan Caulkins, *Modelling the Domestic Distribution Network for Illicit Drugs*, Santa Monica, California: RAND, 1998.
191 Jonathan P. Caulkins and Peter Reuter, *What Price Data Tell Us About Drug Markets*, Pittsburgh, Pennsylvania: Working Paper, H. John Heinz III School of Public Policy and Management, Carnegie-Mellon University, 1998.
192 Source: *Crime in the United States*, FBI, annual, Uniform Crime Reports (arrests) and *What America's Users Spend on Illegal Drugs, 1988-1998*, Office of National Drug Control Policy 2000 (consumption).
193 Source: *Crime in the United States*, FBI, annual, Uniform Crime Reports (arrests) and *What America's Users Spend on Illegal Drugs, 1988-1998*, Office of National Drug Control Policy 2000 (street price).

Heroin: The Case for Prescription

194 John DiNardo, *Law Enforcement, the Price of Cocaine and Cocaine Use*, Santa Monica, California, RAND Corporation, 1998.
195 For the classic account of controlled heroin use, cf. N.E. Zinberg, *Drug, Set, and Setting: The Basis of Controlled Intoxicant Use*, New Haven: Yale University Press, 1984.
196 Source: Wolfgang Heckmann et. al., *Drogennot- und todesfalle. Eine differentielle Untersuchung der Pravalenz und Atiologie der Drogenmortalitat. Schriftenreihe des Bundesministeriums fur Gesundheit*, Band 28, Baden-Baden, 1993, p. 123.
197 Karl-Hans Hartwig and Ingo Pies, *Rationale Drogenpolitik in der Demokratie*, Tübingen: Wirtschaftswissenschaftliche und wirtschaftsethische Perspektiven, 1995, p. 34.
198 Cf. Geoffrey Pearson, *The New Heroin Users*, Oxford: Blackwell, 1987 and Howard Parker, Judith Aldridge and Roy Egginton eds., *UK Drugs Unlimited: New Research and Policy Lessons on Illicit Drug Use*, Houndsmill: Palgrave, 2001. Cf. also the essay by Donald McCarthy in this volume.
199 Arthur Kreuzer, Ruth Römer-Klees, Hans Schneider, 'Beschaffungskriminalität Drogenabhängiger', *BKA-Forschungsreihe*, vol. 24, 1991, pp. 161-168.
200 Cf. Jon Elster ed., *Getting Hooked: Rationality and Addiction*, Cambridge: Cambridge University Press, 1999
201 Cf. the essay in this book by Donald McCarthy for data on the falling street price of heroin
202 Ambros Uchtenhagen, Felix Gutzwiller and Anja Dobler-Mikola eds., *Programme for a Medical Prescription of Narcotics: Final Report of the Research Representatives*, Institut for Sozial-und-Praeventivmedizin der Universitaet Zuerich, 1997, p. 4.
203 *Report of the External Panel on the Evaluation of the Swiss Scientific Studies of Medically Prescribed Narcotics to Drug Addicts*, World Health Organisation, April 1999, Paragraph 5.1.
204 Ambros Uchtenhagen, Felix Gutzwiller and Anja Dobler-Mikola eds., *op. cit.*, p. 6.
205 Source: Ambros Uchtenhagen, Felix Gutzwiller and Anja Dobler-Mikola eds., *op. cit.*
206 *Report of the External Panel on the Evaluation of the Swiss Scientific Studies of Medically Prescribed Narcotics to Drug Addicts*, World Health Organisation, April 1999, Paragraph 5.2.
207 Andreas Frei, Roger-Axel Greiner, Angelika Mehnert, Rolf Dinkel, 'Sozioökonomische Bewertung der Versuche zur ärztlichen Verschreibung von Betäubungsmitteln', *Schlussbericht der HealthEcon AG*, vol. 49, Zurich: Forschungsbericht aus dem Institut für Suchtforschung, 1997, p. 111.
208 Peter Edwards, *They Don't Become Angels*, A research project funded by the Australia-Britain Society, the Australian National Drug Crime Prevention Fund and the Tasmania Police, February 1997.